*Law*Basics

CONSTITUTIONAL LAW

AUSTRALIA
Law Book Co.
Sydney

CANADA and USA
Carswell
Toronto

HONG KONG
Sweet & Maxwell Asia

NEW ZEALAND
Brookers
Wellington

SINGAPORE and MALAYSIA
Sweet & Maxwell Asia
Singapore and Kuala Lumpur

*Law*Basics

CONSTITUTIONAL LAW

Third edition

by

Jane Munro

Advocate,
Former Lecturer in Law, University of Edinburgh

THOMSON

™

W. GREEN

Published in 2005 by

W. Green & Son Ltd
21 Alva Street
Edinburgh EH2 4PS

www.wgreen.thomson.com

Printed in Great Britain by Ashford Colour Press

No natural forests were destroyed to make this product;
Only farmed timber was used and replanted

A CIP catalogue record for this book is available from the British Library

ISBN 0 414 01586 X

CONTENTS

TABLE OF CASES

1. THE UNITED KINGDOM CONSTITUTION

INTRODUCTION

As the term "the United Kingdom constitution" implies, constitutions and constitutional law are linked in a strong sense to the state. But constitutional lawyers must recognise the dimensions of constitutional law that exist beyond the state, *e.g.* Community law and aspects of international law; and those which obtain at a sub-state level, *e.g.* devolution. Perhaps more than most, Scots lawyers are aware of these different dimensions as a result of the distinctive system of Scots law and the changes wrought by the establishment of a Scottish Parliament in 1999.

Despite its historical inheritance, the United Kingdom has a *unitary* constitution (or *union* constitution, a term preferred by some), characterised by a single sovereign legislature and a central government. This model of constitutional organisation may be contrasted with the *federal* constitutions of, *e.g.* Germany, Canada and the United States (and, for that matter, the European Union: it may already be true to say that the unitary constitution of the United Kingdom has been absorbed within a European federation). Federal systems are characterised by the entrenched allocation of powers to the central or federal government on the one hand and to regional governments (of *Länder*, provinces or states) on the other. Within their limits, the central and regional governments are independent of one another, in contrast to the hierarchical relationship between central and local government in the United Kingdom. The distribution of powers in a federation, which is invariably contained in a written constitution, is monitored by a supreme court, which ensures that the regional units do not trespass on federal powers and vice versa.

Short of federalism, systems of devolved or decentralised government are not uncommon even within unitary states. The arguments for decentralisation are both practical and principled. National, ethnic or linguistic distinctions within a state may underpin decentralised forms of government, as in Spain. Central authorities may choose to concede some measure of regional autonomy not only to recognise such distinctions but also in order to prevent them from founding claims to independence and secession. In principle, the concept of *subsidiarity* holds that decisions ought to be taken at a level as close as possible to the citizens affected by them. The concept is recognised in the constitutional law of a number of states (*e.g.* Article 72(2) of the German Basic Law). It has also been recognised as a fundamental principle of Community law by the European Court of Justice, and is now enshrined in Article 5 of the EC Treaty. But subsidiarity is more than an expression of desire for greater "grass roots" democracy. It also acknowledges the fact that many governmental activities are more efficiently and effectively undertaken at a regional or local level than at the centre.

Even prior to devolution, the United Kingdom departed in various ways from the strict model of unitary statehood, in a way going beyond the well-established structure of local authorities. Special provision was made within Parliament for Scotland, and the Secretary of State for Scotland and the former Scottish Office represented a substantial degree of administrative devolution. The Scottish, English and Northern Irish legal systems remain distinct. The establishment of a devolved Scottish Parliament, together with devolved administrations in Wales and Northern Ireland, may prove to have unleashed a dynamic which in time will move the United Kingdom still further away from the model of unitary statehood in the direction of federalism, if not independence for the United Kingdom's constituent countries.

At one level, constitutional law is about institutions, their powers and functions, and the relationships between them. At another level, it is about the relationship between the state and its emanations on the one hand and individual citizens on the other, in particular the rights and liberties of the individual as against the state. Many constitutional systems provide the rules defining and regulating these subjects in a written document or documents. The United Kingdom—even still—does not. British constitutional law consists of a diverse collection of rules and practices including statutes and case law, political practice and the procedures established by different institutions of the state to regulate their own tasks, *e.g.* the law and custom of Parliament. In recent years, however, many key areas of constitutional law have been "committed to paper". The Scotland Act 1998 is one instance of this. Equally important is the Human Rights Act 1998, which incorporated into national law the principal fundamental rights enshrined in the European Convention on Human Rights (ECHR) and which gave us a charter of positive rights directly enforceable before the domestic courts.

As such, constitutional law is a vast and complex subject, confined not merely to legislation and cases but extending to legal and political theory, history, and modern political science. The aim of this book is not to cover the whole field of constitutional law, but to provide a basic guide to some of the more important aspects of the subject in a way which illustrates its diversity without overwhelming, or depressing, those who are trying to make sense of it.

It should be noted that throughout this book, the term "Acts of Parliament" means Acts of the Westminster Parliament. Acts of the Scottish Parliament are referred to as such. The law is as stated at May 2, 2005.

SOURCES OF CONSTITUTIONAL LAW

Legislation

Many Acts of Parliament have special constitutional significance (although they did, until recently, enjoy a higher status as a consequence). Some examples will suffice:

- The Claim of Right 1689 of the Scottish Parliament and the Bill of Rights 1688 of the English Parliament, which contained the terms on which the thrones of James VII of Scotland and II of England, vacated following the Glorious Revolution of 1688, were offered to William and Mary. These statutes laid the foundations of the modern constitution by establishing parliamentary supremacy and rejecting the claims of the Stuart kings to rule by prerogative right.
- The Acts of Union, whereby the Scottish and English Parliaments dissolved themselves in order to unite as one in terms of the Treaty of Union in 1707.
- The Great Reform Act 1832, which laid the foundations of today's democratic franchise. The franchise is now defined in the Representation of the People Act 1983 as amended, most recently by the Representation of the People Act 2000. Important provision is made in relation to the conduct of elections and the regulation of political parties by the Political Parties, Elections and Referendums Act 2000.
- The Parliament Acts of 1911 and 1949, which made it possible to dispense in certain circumstances with the consent of the House of Lords in the enactment of Acts of Parliament.
- The European Communities Act 1972, which incorporated Community law into the legal systems of the United Kingdom and made it possible for the United Kingdom to fulfil the further obligations of membership of what is now the European Union.
- The Scotland Act 1998, the Government of Wales Act 1998 and the Northern Ireland Act 1998, which provided for, respectively, the Scottish Parliament, the National Assembly for Wales and the Northern Ireland Assembly.
- The Human Rights Act 1998, which incorporated into national law the "Convention rights".

Judicial decisions

The judges expound and apply the common law in their decisions in particular cases. Through the mouthpiece of the common law, the courts have provided authoritative (because binding on lower courts by the doctrine of precedent) clarification on a number of areas of constitutional significance, *e.g.* the existence and extent of prerogative powers claimed by the Crown; the legality of governmental acts and the remedies available to citizens injured by illegal acts; and indeed the existence and nature of the fundamental principle of the United Kingdom constitution, parliamentary supremacy.

Bear in mind the following:

- There are still areas of the law governed solely by the common law, but today the intervention of statutes means that the role of the courts is less creative than interpretive. However, the function of interpreting statutes is constitutionally important too. It is by no means a mechanical and self-executing task, and it has been said that the courts may even "supply the omission of the legislature" where this is necessary. For example, in *R v Home Secretary, ex parte Fayed* (1997), the court quashed the Home Secretary's refusal of an application for citizenship, holding that even though the British Nationality Act 1981 exempted the Home Secretary from giving reasons for his decisions, he was still bound to act fairly in the exercise of statutory discretions and that duty might extend to giving reasons.

- The common law is subordinate to statute law, so judicial decisions may be overturned or amended by Act of Parliament.

- Community law overrides the common law, and indeed Acts of Parliament. Where incompatibility exists between Community law and an Act of Parliament, the domestic courts are entitled to make a declaration of incompatibility: *R v Secretary of State for Employment, ex parte Equal Opportunities Commission* (1995). (In terms of section 29 of the Scotland Act 1998, the Scottish Parliament cannot validly legislate in a manner incompatible with Community law. If its enactments breach Community law, the courts are not confined to making declarations of incompatibility but may strike the legislation down.)

- The European Court of Human Rights may hold that national judicial decisions are incompatible with the ECHR. If so, the United Kingdom comes under an international legal obligation to amend national law so as to achieve consistency with the Convention. For some time now the courts have sought to develop the common law in accordance with the requirements of the European Convention. By virtue of section 6(3)(a) of the Human Rights Act 1998, the courts are now *obliged* to do so. Where judicial interpretation of statutes is concerned, section 3 of the Human Rights Act 1998 obliges all courts and tribunals to read and give effect to primary and secondary legislation, so far as possible, consistently with the Convention rights. If this is not practically possible, certain higher courts may, under section 4 of the Human Rights Act, make a declaration of incompatibility in respect of the provision(s) in question, although this has no effect on the "validity, continuing operation or enforcement" of the provision(s) in respect of which it is made. (Again, the position differs in relation to Acts of the Scottish Parliament, which are void if incompatible with the Convention rights.)

Constitutional conventions

In *The Law of the Constitution*, Dicey spoke of "conventions, understandings, habits or practices which, though they may regulate the conduct of the several members of the sovereign power ... are not in reality laws at all since they are not enforced by the courts".

This refers to the many rules of constitutional behaviour which are found neither in statutes nor in judicial decisions but which are nonetheless observed by such constitutional actors as the Queen, the Prime Minister and Cabinet, parliamentarians and judges. There is some dispute about whether these non-legal rules, or constitutional conventions, are prescriptive (saying what ought to happen) or merely descriptive (saying what does happen). Conventions are, at least, descriptive, because fundamentally they are rules of practice, founded on consistent patterns of constitutional behaviour. To take some examples:

- The Sovereign has, in strict legal terms, the power to refuse the Royal Assent to a Bill passed by the House of Commons and the House of Lords, but by convention the Sovereign must always give the Royal Assent on the advice of her ministers. Even when the Royal Assent was last refused—by Queen Anne, to the Scottish Militia Bill in 1708—it seems to have been done on ministerial advice.
- Convention also requires that the Queen exercise her power to appoint ministers on the advice of the Prime Minister, and that ministers should be drawn from Parliament.
- By convention, Her Majesty's government must have the confidence of the House of Commons. Thus when the government loses the confidence of a majority in the House of Commons—as Mr Callaghan's Labour government did in 1979—it must by convention resign.

To argue that a convention is prescriptive implies that what ought to be done, according to the convention, may be enforced. But there is no remedy for breach of a convention in the courts: *Attorney General v Jonathan Cape Ltd* (1976). This does not mean that the courts take no cognisance of conventions when deciding on questions of law, *e.g.* the courts may exercise only low-level control over executive action in areas traditionally subject to political control through the scrutiny of Parliament and the convention of ministerial responsibility (*R v Environment Secretary, ex parte Nottinghamshire C.C.* (1986)). The courts cannot, however, adjudicate on the existence and allegation of breach of a convention, simply because conventions are non-legal rules.

If the courts can provide no remedy, are there any sanctions for breach of a convention; and if not, why are they obeyed at all? It has been said that the reasons for obedience are positive and negative. In the positive sense, conventions are obeyed because they reflect prevailing constitutional values: it is appropriate that what a convention prescribes is done. In the negative sense, conventions are obeyed because political difficulties—even constitutional crises—may flow from disobedience.

However, it is well to be cautious when speaking of "breaches" of conventions. It would be difficult to draw up a list of conventions with which everyone would agree. The degree of obligatoriness of conventions is variable. At one end of the spectrum, there are those usages which have been observed for centuries and which are acknowledged as binding; at the other end, there are relatively new strands of constitutional practice which may or may not, in time, harden into rules. As Turpin remarks, "conventions are always emerging, crystallising and dissolving, and it is sometimes questionable whether a convention has been broken or has simply changed".

Thus the term "breach" may be apposite in the case of well-established conventions, such as that which requires the Queen to act on the advice of her ministers. But even here, there may be exceptional circumstances where it might not be unconstitutional for the Queen to act without, or even in the face of, ministerial advice. In other cases, bear in mind that conventions are essentially rules of practice, and it is a virtue of conventions that they may evolve as practice adjusts to meet new circumstances and changing constitutional values. For example, the traditional convention of ministerial responsibility to Parliament, whereby ministers must accept responsibility for all that takes place within their departments and resign in the event of mistakes or maladministration, may well have altered in the light of contemporary constitutional practice.

Given the lack of clarity surrounding conventions, it might be argued that they should be codified or enacted as legal rules. There are problems with this view. First, codification would be fraught with difficulty. That in itself might not matter if the overall exercise were worth it. But, secondly, even written constitutions cannot provide for every eventuality in the form of legal rules. Codifying conventions would not remove the "penumbra of doubt" which surrounds all rules, legal or non-legal. The need would remain for certain usages and understandings to guide constitutional actors in their interpretation and application of the rules. Thirdly, the very nature of conventions as rules founded on consistent constitutional practice allows for the gradual evolution of the constitutional order as adaptation is necessary, without the need for new legislation or constitutional amendment. One might be suspicious of the degree of flexibility which flows from our reliance on conventions, but all constitutional systems must permit some elasticity if they are to be workable.

Other sources

We have noted the principal sources of constitutional law, but there are others which should be mentioned for completeness. The law and custom of Parliament is one. Parliament's exclusive authority over its own procedures, composition and internal affairs was asserted in the Bill of Rights 1688. (In the Scottish Parliament, these matters are regulated partly by the Scotland Act and associated secondary legislation, and partly by the standing orders of the Scottish Parliament.) The standing orders of the Houses of Parliament, resolutions, rulings of the Speaker and other aspects of parliamentary practice are the source of a number of important constitutional rules and understandings.

Scots law also regards the statements of the institutional writers, such as Stair, Erskine and Hume, as an authoritative source of law in the absence of subsequent contrary authority. English law does not treat legal literature as authoritative as such, but the influence of certain textbooks, *e.g.* Dicey's *The Law of the Constitution* and Erskine May's *Parliamentary Practice*, should not be underestimated.

Having looked at the sources of constitutional law and gained some idea of the nature of the subject, we move on next to the main institutions of the constitution. This is now a two-tier business, with a Scottish Parliament as well as the Westminster Parliament, and a Scottish Executive as well as the central government of the United Kingdom. There is also the judicial system, which is partly distinctive to Scotland and partly shared with the rest of the United Kingdom. It is also necessary to consider the principles of constitutional government which presently form part of British constitutional law and will continue to do so, at least for the time being: parliamentary supremacy, the rule of law and the separation of powers. We then look at constitutional law not from the viewpoint of institutions but from the viewpoint of the individual citizen and his relationship with the state. That relationship was greatly changed by the passage of the Human Rights Act 1998. This has had, and will continue to have, a profound impact on all areas of civil liberty— including, for the purposes of this book, the powers of the police and the law relating to freedom of assembly and public order—and on the judicial review of administrative action.

---

2. WESTMINSTER

THE MEETING OF PARLIAMENT

The meeting of Parliament involves the exercise of prerogative power as qualified by statute and convention. Parliament is summoned and dissolved by royal proclamation; it is also the Sovereign who prorogues Parliament, *i.e.* brings each annual session to an end. But the Sovereign cannot exercise these powers at will. In response to the efforts of the Stuart kings to do so, Article 13 of the Bill of Rights 1688 provided that "Parliament ought to be held frequently". In fact, Parliament has met annually since 1689. The Parliament Act 1911 provides that no Parliament shall last for more than five years, which period begins to run on the date appointed for Parliament to meet after a general election.

THE COMPOSITION OF PARLIAMENT

The Sovereign

We have noted the role of the Sovereign in summoning, proroguing and dissolving Parliament. The Queen is also a part of Parliament, in a formal sense, in that strictly speaking Acts of Parliament are Acts of the Queen in Parliament. Bills approved by the House of Commons and House of Lords must receive the Royal Assent in order to become law, although by convention the Sovereign never refuses the Royal Assent.

The House of Lords

Prior to the entry into force of the House of Lords Act 1999, the House of Lords had 1,330 members—26 archbishops and bishops of the Church of England, 542 life peers appointed under the Life Peerages Act 1958, and 762 hereditary peers. Section 1 of the 1999 Act provided that "no-one shall be a member of the House of Lords by virtue of a hereditary peerage". Section 2 then disapplied this exclusion in relation to 90 hereditary peers elected by the House to continuing membership (for life, or until an Act of Parliament is passed implementing further reform of the House) and 2 hereditary peers holding the offices of Earl Marshal and Lord Great Chamberlain. Section 3 of the Act abolished the disqualifications barring hereditary peers (other than those elected to continuing membership of the House of Lords) from voting in elections to the House of Commons and from standing for election to or being a member of the House of Commons.

The 1999 Act was seen as but the first step in a continuing programme of reform, but the programme has stalled. The Royal Commission on Reform of the House of Lords published a report on longer-term reform of the upper House in January 2000, and its recommendations were endorsed by the government in a White Paper published after the 2001 election. Shortly stated, the White Paper proposed to abolish altogether the right of hereditary peers to sit in the upper House. For the future, the majority of its members would be nominated by political parties in rough proportion to their shares of the national vote at the previous general election. Additional members would be elected to represent the constituent nations and regions of the UK, with a similar number of politically-unaffiliated appointees. An independent Appointments Commission would be established by statute (in place of the appointments body set up by the Prime Minister in 2000) to vet the appointment of independent members. In due course, membership would be capped at 600. The overriding objective was to maintain the respective roles and authority of the two chambers.

These proposals were decisively rejected in a public consultation exercise, and the government placed the matter in the hands of a joint committee of both Houses of Parliament charged with finding a way through to the next stage of reform. In its first report the committee identified seven options for the composition of a reformed second chamber—various combinations of elected and appointed membership between the two extremes of fully elected and fully appointed—all of which were in their turn rejected in a free vote in both the Commons and the Lords in February 2003. The government presented a fresh set of proposals for consultation in September 2003, but in the face of continued, and determined, opposition has chosen to "reflect on the possible options for longer-term reform of the House of Lords, and to encourage wide-ranging debate on the best way forward".

However House of Lords reform resolves itself, the changes to date represent an historic shift in the composition of the House of Lords. For more than a century, attempts of varying degrees of significance have been made to alter the nature of the second chamber of the Westminster Parliament. Note in particular the Parliament Act 1911, which first enabled the House of Commons to dispense with the consent of the Lords to legislation in certain circumstances, and the Parliament Act 1949, which reduced the Lords' delaying power from two years to one.

The House of Commons
Following the 2005 general election, there are 646 MPs, of whom 59 represent Scottish constituencies. The composition of the Commons in party political terms is the consequence of the electoral system currently in use for parliamentary elections in the UK, namely the relative majority or "first past the post" (FPTP) system whereby the candidate who receives the most votes in a constituency—even if it is only one more than the runner-up—is elected to the seat. The Liberal Democrats in particular, being the traditional victims of this system, have long called for its replacement with a system of proportional representation.

There are a number of variations on the theme. The *single transferable vote system* (STV), based on multi-member constituencies in which the voter expresses his preferences for the candidates in numerical order, is used in Northern Ireland for local elections, elections to the European Parliament and elections to the Northern Ireland Assembly under the Northern Ireland Act 1998. The *additional member system* (AMS) seeks to achieve a closer relationship between votes cast and seats won whilst retaining some of the advantages of first-past-the-post, such as the MP/constituency link, lost by STV. It is used in elections to the Scottish Parliament and Welsh Assembly and is explained in the next chapter. The *alternative vote system* (AV), like FPTP, works on the basis of single-member constituencies but, like STV, requires the voter to rank the candidates named on his ballot paper in order of preference. If a candidate obtains more than half of the "first preference" votes, he or she is elected to represent the constituency. If no candidate achieves more than 50 per cent on the first count, the votes of the candidate receiving the lowest number of first preferences are eliminated and his supporters' second preferences are redistributed appropriately. This process continues until one candidate secures an overall majority of votes—more than half—compared to the other candidates. Something like AV was recommended as a replacement for FPTP by the Independent Commission on the Voting System in 1998. But the majority secured by the winning candidate under AV may be a majority in only the loosest sense of the word, and studies have shown that it is capable of producing even more disproportionate representation than the present system. Perhaps unsurprisingly then, the Commission's recommendations went unimplemented.

There are a number of categories of disqualification from membership of the House of Commons (see generally the House of Commons (Disqualification) Act 1975), including those under the age of 21, mental patients, bankrupts and those convicted of a criminal offence carrying a custodial sentence of more than one year. Peers, formerly disqualified, are now entitled to seek election to the House of Commons by virtue of the House of Lords Act 1999. The House of Commons (Removal of Clergy Disqualification) Act 2001 provides that no person shall be disqualified from being or being elected as a member of the House of Commons merely because he has been ordained or is a minister of any religious denomination, although the 26 Lords Spiritual who sit in the House of Lords continue to be disqualified.

THE FUNCTIONS OF PARLIAMENT

Providing and sustaining a government

In the United Kingdom we have a parliamentary executive: the government is drawn from, and responsible to, Parliament. The Sovereign is bound by convention to appoint as Prime Minister the person who appears best able to command the confidence of the Commons, and to invite that person to form a government. As a rule, that person is the leader of the party having an overall majority of seats in the Commons. It is the endorsement of elected MPs that confers democratic legitimacy on the government and its legislation. Therefore, when it appears that the government has lost the confidence of the Commons (usually on a motion of confidence), convention obliges the government to resign. Note, however, that, in modern constitutional practice, defeat in a vote on a government bill is not taken to signify loss of confidence in the government unless the bill is of a sort which is still treated as a matter of confidence by convention (*e.g.* the annual Finance Bills) or unless the government expressly states that the vote is to be treated as a matter of confidence.

This does not mean that a government cannot be formed unless one party secures an overall majority of seats, and indeed, from time to time, government majorities may be dispensed with, as where private members' bills are left to a free vote. However, a minority government is always in a precarious position, and it is unlikely to be long before a general election is advised or forced (*e.g.* having taken office as a minority Prime Minister in February 1974, Mr Wilson called a second election in October 1974). A minority government may forestall the inevitable loss of confidence for a time by entering into agreements with other parties, such as the "Lib-Lab Pact" of 1977 to 1978, which sustained Mr Callaghan's minority administration. However, such arrangements have tended to prove unstable.

Some find repugnant the fact that MPs tend to place party loyalty (a loyalty firmly reinforced by the Whip system) above their role as parliamentarians. It is unsurprising, however, that this is the case, and it is pointless to suggest reforms which no government will introduce, *e.g.* secret voting instead of the present system of voting by walking through the division lobbies. The current position is to a great extent the product of the present electoral system—by and large, a two-horse race which tends to produce majority governments of one stripe or another and therefore emphasises the importance of party cohesion.

Legislation

Parliament is the primary legislative institution in the UK and Acts of Parliament are the highest form of law. The enactment of an Act of Parliament begins with the laying of a bill before one of the two Houses of Parliament. The bill then undergoes a process of scrutiny in both Houses, at the end of which Commons and Lords must agree on the final text, although it is possible for the Commons to dispense with the agreement of the Lords in certain circumstances. The bill then receives the Royal Assent and thus becomes an Act of Parliament.

Bills fall into two categories: *private bills* and *public bills*. Erskine May defines private bills as "bills of a special kind, for conferring particular powers or benefits on any person or body of persons ... in excess of or in conflict with the general law". They are introduced in Parliament by parliamentary agents acting on behalf of the prospective beneficiary of the legislation. After their second reading in each House, they are considered by a select committee, which considers whether the special powers sought are in order and in line with precedent. Any objectors to the bill are entitled to be heard by the committee before it decides whether or not to accept it.

Public bills relate to matters of general public interest and are introduced either by an MP or a peer. All government legislation is enacted by means of public bills. *Government bills* are sponsored by a minister and occupy the greater part of parliamentary time each session. *Private members' bills*, whereby backbench MPs may propose legislation, undergo essentially the same procedure as government bills but are more likely to fail for lack of time unless supported, at least tacitly, by the government.

The first formal stage of the legislative process is the *first reading*, where the bill is announced to Parliament. At *second reading*, the bill is explained to the House in which it was introduced—it is assumed in the following account that this is the House of Commons, but bills may equally be introduced in the Lords—and debated. If the principles of the bill are opposed, a vote follows the debate, and if the bill is defeated (as is usual for private members' bills, but very rare for government bills) it proceeds no further.

The bill is then sent for detailed scrutiny by a *standing committee* of some 20 MPs selected to reflect the party balance in the House. Bills of special significance may be examined by a *committee of the whole House*. It may be amended at this stage.

The *report stage* follows the completion of the committee's task, when the bill is "reported" to the House. Further amendments may be tabled for debate at the report stage, although usually few of these can be addressed in the time available. Bills considered by a committee of the whole House also have a report stage if amended at second reading; otherwise, they proceed directly to *third reading*.

At third reading, the bill is debated in its final form. It then proceeds to the House of Lords. The procedure in the Lords is like that in the Commons, except that the committee stages are usually taken on the floor of the Lords. The Lords rarely vote on any of the readings of a government bill, and there is no provision for foreclosing debate in the Lords. In the Commons, by contrast, where timetabling is more of a problem, *programme motions* or *allocation of time (guillotine) motions* may be moved, debated and voted upon by the House. These fix the time available for each stage of a bill, and can considerably cut down the opportunities for scrutiny.

If the Lords make no amendments to a bill, it is automatically submitted for the Royal Assent. If amendments have been made, the bill returns to the Commons, which may agree to the amendments, substitute amendments of its own, or reject the amendments outright. In the latter two cases, the bill is sent back to the Lords accompanied by the Commons' reasons. As a rule, the Lords will accept the decision of the Commons. Occasionally, however, they stand their ground. In most such cases, compromise will eventually be reached, but, exceptionally, the two Houses will fail to reach agreement on a final text within the parliamentary session. In that event, subject to the provisions of the Parliament Acts 1911 and 1949, the bill usually lapses. Under the Parliament Acts, the House of Lords has no power to amend or delay a bill certified by the Speaker to be a money bill. The Lords can delay any other public bill for one session, but it is open to the Commons to revive the bill in the next session, leapfrog the Lords and proceed directly to the Royal Assent. The Lords do, however, retain a power of veto over private bills, statutory instruments and bills to extend the life of Parliament beyond its current five-year term. The Parliament Acts procedure has been used more frequently in recent years. Following its deployment to secure the passing of the Hunting Act 2004, a group of hunt supporters challenged the validity of the Parliament Act 1949, and accordingly also of the 2004 Act: *R (Jackson) v HM Attorney General* (2005). The Court of Appeal accepted that the Parliament Act 1911 could not have been used to effect a fundamental constitutional resettlement, such as the abolition of the House of Lords, but held that the reduction in the delaying period from two years to one was competent under the 1911 Act, and that the 1949 and 2004 Acts were valid accordingly.

Although the legislative process occupies a great deal of parliamentary time, the effectiveness of parliamentary scrutiny of government legislation is limited. It might at a very general level be said that the smaller the majority enjoyed by a government, the more vulnerable are its legislative intentions to amendment if not outright defeat, although in recent years a government blessed with a substantial majority has more than once encountered difficulty in getting its proposals past the Commons, to say nothing of the Lords. Ultimately, whether the government's majority is large or small, there is much truth in the view that "Parliament's role is one of registration and legitimation: it cloaks legislation agreed elsewhere with the form and force of law". Certain efforts have been made to address the perceived deficiencies of parliamentary scrutiny, including greater use of pre-legislative consultation on the policies and principles of legislative proposals and advance programming of a bill's progress through Parliament. Concern remains that the sheer pressure of parliamentary business will continue to prevent proper consideration of legislative proposals without a more radical review of the way that business is handled.

Scrutiny of the executive
To the extent that most of the legislative business of Parliament involves government legislation, the legislative process itself provides some scope for scrutiny of the executive. But a number of alternative procedural mechanisms exist to facilitate and enforce the government's responsibility to Parliament for its acts and decisions. *Parliamentary questions* take place every day when the Commons are sitting, except Friday. Most answers given by ministers at these times are in response to earlier, written questions (and questions for written answer may be put at any time), but the MP concerned may raise oral supplementary questions based on the minister's reply. Over 40,000 questions are put down for answer in every session of Parliament. *Adjournment debates* take place each day at the close of public business in the Commons, although they are unlikely to have much impact as ministers have advance notice of the subject of debate and time to prepare their defences. MPs may move for an adjournment of the House to permit a debate on an urgent issue, but *urgency debates* are rare. The opposition has the opportunity to set the agenda for debates on *opposition days*. But parliamentary committees provide perhaps the most focused opportunities for scrutiny of the executive. Select committees have been a feature of parliamentary life for many years, but the present system of departmental select committees was established only in 1979. These are appointed for the life of each Parliament to examine the expenditure, administration and policy of the main departments and public bodies associated with those departments. Their membership reflects the party balance in the Commons: a majority

of members will be backbench MPs from the government party. This can lead to voting along party lines when the committee decides upon the content of its reports.

As the Select Committee on Procedure asserted in 1990, the new departmental select committees do provide "a far more vigorous, systematic and comprehensive scrutiny of ministers' actions and policies than anything which went before". But the effectiveness of the various mechanisms for parliamentary scrutiny of the executive remains open to question. It may be that developments such as the entry into force of the Freedom of Information Act 2000 on January 1, 2005 will strengthen the ability of MPs to hold the government to account. But deficiencies in scrutiny of the executive are not only the fault of successive governments, anxious not to subtract from their power. MPs themselves have sometimes lacked the will to utilise fully the opportunities for scrutiny which already exist.

SCOTTISH AFFAIRS AT WESTMINSTER

In the past, special arrangements were made for the handling of Scottish business in the House of Commons through the establishment of the Scottish Grand Committee, the Scottish standing committees and the Select Committee on Scottish Affairs, and through time set aside for Scottish questions. Devolution entailed a review of these arrangements. In May 1999, the House of Commons Select Committee on Procedure published a report entitled *The Procedural Consequences of Devolution*. Most of its recommendations for the handling of Scottish, Welsh and Northern Irish matters were implemented by resolution of the House of Commons in October 1999.

The Scottish Grand Committee, a body comprising all Scottish MPs, began life in 1894. Just prior to devolution, its functions included: questions to Scottish Office ministers and Scottish Law Officers (supplementing monthly Scottish Questions in the Commons and the questioning of ministers by the Select Committee on Scottish Affairs), "short debates" on Scottish matters, consideration of the principles of Scottish legislation, debates on negative or affirmative resolutions on statutory instruments, and adjournment debates. Following a recommendation from the Select Committee of Procedure, the Grand Committee was suspended in the run up to devolution. But the government was uneasy about abolishing it altogether on the grounds that, even after devolution, Scottish MPs would wish to hold debates on matters reserved to Westminster for which time could not be found on the floor of the House of Commons itself. The Commons therefore resolved to retain the Grand Committee, and it has continued to meet from time to time since it "reconvened" in February 2000.

At present there are two Scottish standing committees at Westminster. They may consist of between 16 and 50 MPs, and at least 16 must represent Scottish constituencies. Their task is to undertake the committee stages of bills certified by the Speaker of the House of Commons as relating exclusively to Scotland.

The Select Committee on Scottish Affairs was established in October 1979 as part of the wider reform of the select committee system at Westminster. Its purpose is to examine, on behalf of the House of Commons, the expenditure, administration and policy of the Scotland Office and associated public authorities and, from time to time, the policies of United Kingdom government departments as these affect Scotland. It has 11 members, not all of whom need represent Scottish constituencies.

Following the establishment of the Scottish Parliament, the House of Commons resolved that the range of parliamentary questions that might properly be put to Scotland Office ministers should be reduced to matters relating to their ministerial responsibilities. Questions may not therefore be tabled on matters for which responsibility has been devolved unless the question seeks information which the United Kingdom government is empowered to require of the Scottish Executive, matters included in legislation to be introduced in the United Kingdom Parliament, matters subject to a concordat between the United Kingdom government and the Scottish Executive, or matters in which United Kingdom government ministers have taken an official interest. The time set aside for Scottish questions has also been reduced: since November 1999, they take place once every four weeks and last for half an hour.

PARLIAMENTARY PRIVILEGE

The privileges of Parliament are rooted in the law and custom of Parliament. At the opening of each new Parliament, the Speaker formally claims from the Crown for the Commons "their ancient rights and privileges", namely, freedom of speech; freedom from arrest; the exclusive right to regulate composition; and exclusive cognisance of internal affairs. Parliament also asserts an exclusive jurisdiction over the existence and extent of its privileges and over breaches of privileges, although this has provoked confrontation with the ordinary courts.

Freedom of speech
This is the most important privilege. Claims to freedom of speech were given a statutory foundation in Article 9 of the Bill of Rights 1688, which provided that "the freedom of speech and debates or proceedings in Parliament ought not to be impeached or questioned in any court or place out of Parliament".

Thus members may not be held liable, as a matter either of civil or criminal law, in respect of words spoken during debates or in the course of parliamentary proceedings, although they may fall foul of the disciplinary jurisdiction of the House itself. In 1938, for example, the privilege protected Duncan Sandys MP from prosecution under the Official Secrets Act 1911 after he disclosed material concerning national security in a parliamentary question. The main effect of the privilege in civil law is the absolute immunity it confers in the law of defamation. In *Church of Scientology v Johnson-Smith* (1972), the Church brought a libel action against Geoffrey Johnson-Smith MP in respect of comments he had made on television. It was held that Mr Johnson-Smith's speeches in the Commons were inadmissible as evidence of malice. Similarly, in *Prebble v TV New Zealand* (1995), the Privy Council rejected TVNZ's argument that, although Article 9 prevented parliamentary proceedings *founding* an action, it did not prevent them being used in support of an action or in its defence. Lord Browne-Wilkinson held that this argument was both inconsistent with authority and with the basic principle upon which the privilege rests—that, so far as possible, MPs should be able to speak freely without fear that what they say might later be used against them in court.

This does not mean that no reference whatsoever may be made in court to parliamentary proceedings. Since 1980, the House of Commons has permitted reference to be made in court to Hansard and published reports of committees. In *Pepper v Hart* (1993), the House of Lords held that the courts might have resort to ministerial statements in Hansard if necessary to clarify ambiguities or to resolve apparent absurdities in legislation, stating that this would not involve "impeaching or questioning" freedom of speech. And an important amendment to Article 9 was made by section 13 of the Defamation Act 1996. This enables MPs to waive their privilege in order to pursue an action for defamation, and was utilised by former MP and minister Neil Hamilton in his abortive libel action against the *Guardian*.

The scope of the privilege is unclear owing to the inexact nature of the term "proceedings in Parliament". In 1938, the House of Commons asserted that the privilege extends to "everything said or done by a member in the exercise of his functions as a member in a committee in either House, as well as everything said or done in either House in the transaction of parliamentary business". Physical location does not provide a conclusive test: it was held in *Rivlin v Bilainkin* (1953) that defamatory letters were not protected merely because they had been posted to MPs within the Palace of Westminster. By the same token, a "proceeding in Parliament" may take place outside, or nowhere near, Parliament, as the Committee of Privileges held in 1968 after a select committee meeting at Essex University was disrupted by protestors.

A difficult case arose in 1958, when George Strauss MP wrote a letter to the Paymaster-General criticising the practices of London Electricity Board. The letter was brought to the attention of the Board, which threatened to sue Mr Strauss for libel unless he retracted his remarks and apologised. Mr Strauss referred the matter to the Committee of Privileges, which found that the letter constituted a "proceeding in Parliament" within the meaning of Article 9. Subsequently, however, the Commons held on a free vote that the letter was not a proceeding in Parliament and that the Board had not, therefore, acted in breach of privilege.

If parliamentary proceedings are protected by Article 9, what of their publication outside Parliament? This question generated one of the great confrontations between Parliament and the courts in 1839 when, by order of the Commons, Hansard published a report stating that an indecent book published by Stockdale was circulating in Newgate Prison. Stockdale sued Hansard in defamation: *Stockdale v Hansard* (1839). The Commons ordered Hansard to plead the authority of the Commons and that the Commons had resolved the case to be one of privilege, which resolution could not be challenged by the courts as each House was the sole judge of its own privileges. The court rejected Hansard's defence. It was held that mere resolutions of the House could not change the law, and that it was for the court to determine the existence and extent of parliamentary privileges when their assertion affected individuals outside Parliament. Here, privilege did not extend to permitting publication of defamatory material outside of Parliament.

The decision in *Stockdale v Hansard* led to the enactment of the Parliamentary Papers Act 1840, which statutorily extends the protection of absolute privilege from civil or criminal proceedings to papers published under the authority of Parliament as certified by an officer of either House. Qualified privilege applies to publications of fair and accurate reports of parliamentary papers, so that there is no liability in defamation without proof of malice.

Freedom from arrest

This privilege protects members from civil arrest, but not from arrest in connection with criminal offences. Since the abolition of imprisonment for debt in the late 19th century, the privilege has had little significance. However, it was held in *Stourton v Stourton* (1963) that a member (in this case, a peer who had failed to comply with a maintenance order) is immune from committal for contempt of court where imprisonment is sought in order to enforce performance of a civil obligation. Collateral privileges flow from the basic principle underlying freedom from arrest, namely the right of Parliament to the uninterrupted attendance and services of its members, *e.g.* exemption from jury service.

Exclusive right to regulate composition

Formerly, the most important aspect of this privilege lay in the Commons' right to determine the result of disputed parliamentary elections. This jurisdiction has now been transferred by statute to the courts. The Houses of Parliament do, however, retain the right to determine whether a person is disqualified from membership of either House. Thus in 1960, the Commons declared vacant the seat of Tony Benn MP when he succeeded to a viscountcy on the death of his father and barred him from the chamber. The Commons may also expel a member on grounds other than disqualification, *e.g.* gross contempt of the House.

Exclusive cognisance of internal affairs

Each House claims the exclusive right to control its own proceedings and to regulate its internal affairs without interference from the courts. By and large, the courts have acquiesced in this privilege. It is one reason why the courts decline to investigate alleged procedural defects when the validity of an Act of Parliament is challenged: *Pickin v British Railways Board* (1974). Similarly, in *Bradlaugh v Gossett* (1884), the court held that it had no jurisdiction to intervene when Mr Bradlaugh, an atheist who had been refused the opportunity of taking the oath required before an MP may sit and vote, contested the legality of a resolution of the House to exclude him and sought an injunction to restrain the Serjeant at Arms from enforcing that resolution.

Penal jurisdiction

The Houses of Parliament retain a jurisdiction to deal with breaches of privilege and contempts. "Contempt of Parliament" is an umbrella term for any offences punishable by the House, namely conduct which offends against the authority and dignity of the House, or, to quote Erskine May: "any act or omission which obstructs or impedes either House in the performance of its functions, or which obstructs or impedes any member or officer of such House in the discharge of his duty, or which has a tendency, directly or indirectly, to produce such results".

"Contempt" therefore includes breaches of privilege, *i.e.* infringements of any of the specific privileges considered above. The distinction between the two may be important, however, for while the Houses cannot extend the scope of their own privileges and questions of the existence and extent of privilege may be addressed by the courts, the list of possible contempts remains open and the courts cannot question the causes of committal for contempt. Thus in the *Case of the Sheriff of Middlesex* (1840), when two sheriffs sought to recover damages owed by Hansard after *Stockdale v Hansard* (1839), the Commons committed Stockdale and the sheriffs for contempt. In *habeas corpus* proceedings to release them, it was held that the ordinary courts had no power but to accept the statement of the House that the committal was for contempt.

Established categories of contempt include disorderly conduct within the precincts of the House; obstruction of members going to or coming from the House, bribery, corruption and other species of dishonesty, and refusal to give evidence before committees of the House. Specific examples may be given. In 1963, Mr John Profumo MP, the Secretary of State for War, was held to have committed contempt by falsely denying before the Commons any association with persons regarded as a security risk. More recently, the actions of a journalist who purported to offer MPs "cash for questions" were held contemptuous, even though a number of MPs accepted.

The fact that conduct is found to constitute contempt does not mean that the House will take further action against the contemnor. The

Commons resolved in 1978 only to use its powers of punishment when "satisfied that to do so is essential to provide reasonable protection for the House, its members or its officers, from such improper obstruction or attempt or threat of obstruction as is causing or is liable to cause substantial interference with the performance of their respective functions". Nevertheless, the range of penalties at the theoretical disposal of the House is considerable. A member may be expelled or suspended; members or "strangers" may be admonished or reprimanded at the Bar of the House. Persons may be committed for contempt, without recourse to the ordinary courts. The House retains a power, last used in 1880, or imprisonment, although it has no power to impose fines.

Reform

Although the rules of parliamentary privilege may sometimes seem archaic, good grounds remain for their existence and application—a point illustrated by provision made in the Scotland Act 1998 to extend aspects of parliamentary privilege to the Scottish Parliament. Nevertheless, in line with its wider mission to modernise the workings of Parliament, the Labour government elected in May 1997 appointed a Joint Committee made up of members of the House of Commons and the House of Lords to review the law and practice of parliamentary privilege and to make recommendations. The Committee published its first report in April 1999. As it stated:

> "[T]he proper functioning of Parliament lies at the heart of a healthy parliamentary democracy. It is in the interests of the nation as a whole that the two Houses of Parliament should have the rights and immunities that they need in order to function properly. But the protection afforded by privilege should be no more than Parliament needs to carry out its functions effectively and to safeguard its constitutional position. Appropriate procedures should exist to prevent abuse and ensure fairness."

The Committee favoured abolition of existing privileges in only a few cases; in particular, freedom from arrest in civil cases. The majority of its proposals involved placing existing privileges in statutory form (see, *e.g.* its recommendation that the terms "proceedings in Parliament" and "place out of Parliament" be defined by statute) or addressing the more obvious anachronisms (as where it recommended the replacement of the Parliamentary Papers Act 1840 with "modern and intelligible legislation"). It also recommended that Parliament's disciplinary and penal powers be reviewed in light of the Convention rights. However, it remains to be seen whether a Parliamentary Privileges Bill will be brought forward to give effect to these recommendations.

3. THE SCOTTISH PARLIAMENT

Devolution was defined by the Report of the Royal Commission on the Constitution in 1973 as "the delegation of central government powers without the relinquishment of sovereignty". This can involve merely the delegation of executive and administrative powers, as to the old Scottish Office after its establishment in 1885. But it can be taken further, to include the delegation of legislative authority, as to the Scottish Parliament pursuant to the Scotland Act 1998.

The Scotland Act brought to fruition a campaign for a Scottish Parliament which, with varying degrees of intensity, had been running since the repeal of the Scotland Act 1978 following the unsuccessful referendum on devolution in March 1979. Shortly after the 1997 general election, legislation was brought forward providing for referendums in Scotland and Wales on whether a Scottish Parliament and Welsh Assembly respectively should be established. The Scottish referendum held on September 11, 1997 posed two questions: whether there should be a Parliament; and whether it should have tax-varying powers. On a turnout of 60 per cent, three-quarters of those who voted were in favour of the first question, and two-thirds were in favour of the second. The Scotland Bill was introduced in the House of Commons in December 1997 and received Royal Assent on November 19, 1998. The first elections to the Parliament took place on May 6, 1999, with the first meeting of the Parliament on May 12. It was officially opened by the Queen on July 1, 1999, on which date also a substantial swathe of executive powers passed from the United Kingdom Government to the new Scottish Executive.

COMPOSITION AND ELECTIONS

The Scotland Act provides that there shall be 129 members of the Scottish Parliament. Seventy three are elected according to the first-past-the-post method used to elect members of the Westminster Parliament, but on the basis of pre-2005 Westminster constituencies. This arrangement is unaffected by the reduction in the number of Scottish Westminster constituencies pursuant to the Scottish Parliament (Constituencies) Act 2004. An MSP may resign his seat at any time simply by giving notice in writing to the Presiding Officer (the near-equivalent in Scotland to the Speaker of the House of Commons). If, by reason of resignation or otherwise, the seat of a constituency member falls vacant, a by-election must be held unless the date of the by-election would fall within three months of the next ordinary general election. Otherwise, it is for the Presiding Officer to appoint the date for the by-election, which must be held within three months of the vacancy arising.

The remaining 56 members are elected in accordance with the additional member system of proportional representation, with seven "regional members" being drawn from each of the eight constituencies provided for by the European Parliamentary Constituencies (Scotland) Order 1996, although for European elections these constituencies have now been supplanted by the electoral system contained in the European Parliamentary Elections Act 1999, under which Scotland constitutes a single region for the purpose of electing its eight MEPs. Candidates for election as a regional member may stand as individual candidates or be named on a regional list submitted by a registered political party of which the candidate is a member. Party lists may have between one and twelve names on them.

Vacancies arising in regional seats are dealt with differently from those in constituency seats. Usually, such a vacancy will be filled by the regional returning officer notifying the Presiding Officer of the name of the next person nominated in the appropriate party's regional list. If the party's regional list is exhausted—because the next names down have changed their minds about being MSPs, perhaps, or if the party failed to take the precaution of nominating the maximum of 12 regional candidates—the seat will simply remain vacant until the next general election. Similarly, if a regional seat allotted to an individual candidate falls vacant, it will not be filled. For practical reasons, the Scotland Act makes no provision for by-elections in these circumstances.

As at Westminster, those falling within the scope of the House of Commons (Disqualification) Act 1975 may not stand for election to the Scottish Parliament. Persons disqualified otherwise than by virtue of the 1975 Act are citizens of foreign countries other than the Republic of Ireland, member states of the Commonwealth and member states of the European Union, persons under the age of 21, those suffering from a mental illness, undischarged bankrupts, convicted prisoners serving a custodial sentence of more than one year, and persons convicted of corrupt or illegal election practices. The Scotland Act made express provision entitling peers other than Lords of Appeal in Ordinary and persons who have been ordained or who are ministers of any religious denomination to stand for election to the Scottish Parliament. At the time, persons falling into either of those categories were disqualified from membership of the House of Commons, although that position has since been changed by the House of Lords Act 1999 and the House of Commons (Removal of Clergy Disqualification) Act 2001.

The Scotland Act provides that ordinary general elections to the Scottish Parliament shall be held on the first Thursday in May every four years. Should that date be unsuitable for some reason, the Presiding Officer may propose an alternative date not more than one month prior to or later than the first Thursday in May. The Queen will then issue a proclamation dissolving the Parliament, requiring the election to be held on the date proposed and requiring the Parliament to meet within seven days of the day following the poll. The Act also provides for extraordinary general elections to be held, on a date proposed by the Presiding Officer, if at least two-thirds of the MSPs vote in favour of a resolution that the Parliament be dissolved; or if the Parliament fails to nominate one of its number as First Minister within 28 days of a general election, the resignation of an incumbent First Minister, that office falling vacant by reason other than resignation, or of the First Minister ceasing to be an MSP otherwise than by reason of a dissolution of the Scottish Parliament. Where an extraordinary general election is held within the six month period prior to the first Thursday in May of a year in which an ordinary election should have taken place, the Act provides that that ordinary election shall not take place. This does not, however, affect the year and timing of subsequent ordinary elections.

LEGISLATIVE COMPETENCE

Making laws for Scotland is not the only, but is certainly the most important, function of the Scottish Parliament. It must be stressed at once, however, that although according to traditional constitutional theory the Westminster Parliament may make or repeal any law whatsoever, the legislative competence of the Scottish Parliament is limited by the Scotland Act. If the Scottish Parliament enacts legislation which has extraterritorial effect, which "relates to" matters reserved to Westminster, which is incompatible with European Community law or with the Convention rights (*i.e.* those rights enshrined in the European Convention on Human Rights which have been incorporated into national law by the Human Rights Act), or which removes the Lord Advocate from his position as head of the systems of criminal prosecution and investigation of deaths in Scotland, section 29 of the Scotland Act makes clear that it "is not law" and is liable as such to be struck down by the courts.

The list of matters reserved to the exclusive competence of the Westminster Parliament is contained in Schedule 5 to the Scotland Act. Any matter absent from that list must be presumed to fall within the competence of the Scottish Parliament. The list may be modified by way of Order in Council as necessary or expedient.

Part I of the Schedule contains a number of General Reservations; namely, the constitution, political parties, foreign affairs, the civil service, defence and treason. Part II sets out Specific Reservations under 11 heads (A to K). These include fiscal, economic and monetary policy; the currency; financial services and financial markets, the law on misuse of drugs, data protection law, electoral law, immigration and nationality, national security, emergency powers, trade and industry policy, including company law, insolvency law, competition law, intellectual property law, import and export control and consumer protection, the post office and postal services, energy, rail, marine and air transport; social security, child support, pensions law, the regulation of certain professions, employment law, abortion, embryology, surrogacy and genetics, broadcasting, and further miscellaneous matters including judicial salaries and equal opportunities.

The precise boundary between reserved and devolved matters is obviously crucial to an understanding of the scope of the Scottish Parliament's legislative competence. Section 29(3) of the Scotland Act provides that the question whether a provision of an Act of the Scottish Parliament relates to a reserved matter "is to be determined ... by reference to the purpose of the provision, having regard (among other things) to its effect in all the circumstances". Modifications of Scots private law or Scots criminal law as they apply to reserved matters are not incompetent provided the object of the provision in question is to make the law apply consistently as between reserved and devolved matters (section 29(4)). Equally, a provision will not be incompetent merely because it has effects on reserved matters which are *incidental to or consequential on* provision made for purposes relating to devolved matters (Schedule 4, paragraph 3). Lastly, section 101 of the Act provides that any provision of an Act of the Scottish Parliament which could be read in such a way as to be outside competence is to be read as narrowly as necessary to bring it within competence, if such a reading is possible, and is to have effect accordingly.

These provisions suggest that a purposive and flexible approach should be taken to the interpretation of Scottish legislation when issues of competence arise. There are other reasons for favouring such an approach. First, the fact that the Scotland Act reserves powers to Westminster instead of transferring limited powers to the Scottish Parliament is indicative of a presumption in favour of the validity of Scottish legislation, rebuttable only if the Parliament clearly strays into reserved areas. Such a presumption is reinforced by the principle of subsidiarity, which provides powerful theoretical justification for an expansive attitude to the competence of the Scottish Parliament.

Legislative competence: pre-Assent checks

However that may be, Scottish legislation is by its very nature vulnerable to legal challenge, both before and after its enactment. The Scotland Act, together with the standing orders of the Scottish Parliament, provides mechanisms for ensuring that any excesses of competence are detected and corrected at as early a stage as possible. First, section 31 of the Act requires the Scottish Minister in charge of a bill to make a statement, on or before the introduction of the bill in the Parliament, that in his view the provisions of the bill are within the legislative competence of the Parliament. Since this requirement is imposed only on members of the Scottish Executive, it can only apply in relation to bills introduced by the Scottish Ministers. However, section 31 also requires the Presiding Officer to decide whether or not in his view the provisions of a bill—of any sort—introduced in the Scottish Parliament are within the competence of the Parliament and to state his decision. A negative statement from the Presiding Officer would not block the onward progress of a bill, but would serve to warn the Parliament of doubts about its *vires*.

Secondly, assuming a bill is passed by the Parliament, it is for the Presiding Officer to submit it for Royal Assent. Section 32 of the Scotland Act, however, provides that he shall not so submit it at any time when the Advocate General, Lord Advocate or Attorney General for England and Wales is entitled to refer the bill to the Judicial Committee of the Privy Council under section 33, when any such reference has been made but has not been decided or otherwise disposed of by the Privy Council, or when an order may be made by the Secretary of State under section 35 prohibiting the submission of the bill for Royal Assent— although this last is not a control over the legislative competence of the Parliament. A reference under section 33 may be made at any time during the four-week period commencing with the passing of a bill by the Parliament, unless the Law Officers notify the Presiding Officer that they do not intend to make a reference. If a reference is made, the Scottish Parliament may choose simply to wait until it has been disposed of. If the Privy Council finds that the bill is *intra vires*, the Presiding Officer may then submit it for Royal Assent without further ado. If not, the bill cannot be sent forward for Royal Assent in unamended form. The Parliament may in that event reconsider the bill in a form designed to rectify the problems with the earlier version.

A reference to the Privy Council may take some considerable time to resolve, however, especially where the bill raises some question of compatibility with European Community law. Although the Privy Council may competently deal with such a question itself, it may decide to refer the matter to the European Court of Justice. In that event, the reference could take years to dispose of. Section 34 of the Scotland Act therefore provides for the Scottish Parliament to resolve to reconsider a bill before any reference, whether to the Privy Council or the Court of Justice, is decided. But even if the Parliament passes the bill in a form amended to take account of the concerns giving rise to the original reference, it may still be the subject of a second reference should one of the Law Officers remain unsatisfied as to its *vires*.

Legislative competence: post-Assent challenges

Even if a bill is passed, receives Royal Assent and enters into force as an Act of the Scottish Parliament, it follows from the fact that it "is not law" if it is outwith competence that its validity remains open to attack in the courts. Such challenges are referred to in the Scotland Act as "devolution issues", and provision is made for these in section 98 and Schedule 6. But the competence and validity of Acts of the Scottish Parliament are not the only species of devolution issue. Others include:

- Questions whether decisions of the Scottish Ministers, First Minister or Lord Advocate are within devolved competence.

- Whether an act or decision of, or a failure to act by, the Scottish Ministers, First Minister or Lord Advocate is incompatible with the Convention rights or with Community law.
- "Any other question about whether a function is exercisable within devolved competence or in or as regards Scotland and any other question arising by virtue of this Act about reserved matters."

Under Part II of Schedule 6, proceedings in Scotland for the determination of a devolution issue may be instituted by the Advocate General or Lord Advocate, but devolution issues may equally be raised, either by way of claim or defence, by any person. For example, a person might seek judicial review in the ordinary way of a Scottish statutory instrument or other act of a member of the Scottish Executive on the grounds that the act falls outwith devolved competence. Alternatively, a person charged with a criminal offence might plead the invalidity of the Scottish legislation under which he is charged, or of the decision to prosecute, by way of defence. The latter approach has characterised many of the leading devolution cases to date, including *Starrs v Ruxton* (2000) and *Stott v Brown* (2001), which concerned the compatibility of prosecution decisions taken on behalf of the Lord Advocate with Article 6 of the ECHR.

It is important to note that, while only the Privy Council has jurisdiction to pronounce on the competence of Scottish legislation prior to its receiving Royal Assent (by way of a section 33 reference), a devolution issue may be raised in any proceedings before any court or tribunal. However, a tribunal from which there is no right of appeal must refer a devolution issue which arises before it to the Inner House of the Court of Session. Other tribunals, and any court other than the House of Lords or a court consisting of three or more judges of the Court of Session, may do so. In criminal matters, a court other than a court consisting of two or more judges of the High Court of Justiciary may refer a devolution issue arising in proceedings before it to the High Court. Where a devolution issue is raised before either the Court of Session or the High Court, they may choose to refer the issue to the Privy Council for resolution. In any event, decisions on devolution issues taken by the Inner House of the Court of Session, a court consisting of two or more judges of the High Court of Justiciary or a court of three or more judges of the Court of Session from which there is no appeal to the House of Lords are appealable, with leave, to the Privy Council. This is significant as, in Scottish criminal causes, there was no right of appeal beyond the High Court in Scotland prior to the enactment of the Scotland Act.

Under paragraph 33 of Schedule 6, the Lord Advocate, Advocate General, Attorney General or Attorney General for Northern Ireland may require any court or tribunal to refer to the Privy Council any devolution issue which has arisen in proceedings before it to which he is a party. In addition, any one of these Law Officers may refer to the Privy Council a devolution issue which is not the subject of legal proceedings. Where this power is exercised in relation to the proposed exercise of a function by a member of the Scottish Executive, that person is disabled from exercising that function in the manner proposed until the reference has been disposed of.

SCOTTISH LEGISLATION

Within the limitations on its competence outlined above, the Scottish Parliament may enact legislation in any one of a number of forms provided for by Chapters 9 and 9A of the standing orders. Chapter 9 lays down general rules applicable to all public bills introduced in the Scottish Parliament, except to the extent that special rules prescribed for particular types of bills are inconsistent with the general rules. In that event, the special rules prevail. Chapter 9A makes provision for private legislation.

The greater part of Scottish legislation originates in *executive bills*; bills introduced by the Scottish Ministers. Apart from the statements by the sponsoring minister and the Presiding Officer as to its *vires*, an executive bill must also be accompanied by a financial memorandum setting out the costs associated with the bill, a policy memorandum explaining the its policy objectives, explanatory notes summarising its purpose and effects, and, if it contains provisions charging expenditure on the Scottish Consolidated Fund, a report signed by the Auditor General for Scotland on whether the charge is appropriate. The general purpose of these accompanying documents is to enhance the transparency of the legislative process and to assist the Parliament and its committees in their task of considering the bill's principles and provisions.

The legislative process following introduction is divided into three stages. At the first stage, the bill is referred to the parliamentary committee within whose remit its subject matter falls. If the bill falls within the remit of more than one committee, one will be designated lead committee. The other committees report to the lead committee, which takes their views into account when it comes to report to the Parliament. The purpose of this stage is to assess the bill's general principles. In doing so, the committee(s) may take evidence from officials in the Scottish Executive and others with an interest or expertise in the issues raised by the bill. At the end of stage one, the Parliament must decide, in the light of the (lead) committee's report, whether the general principles of the bill are agreed to. If so, the bill proceeds to stage two. Here it is subjected to detailed scrutiny and may be amended. Stage two is normally conducted by the committee or lead committee which conducted stage one, although it may be taken by a Committee of the Whole Parliament (convened by the Presiding Officer) if the Parliament so resolves. At the end of stage two, if the bill has been amended, it is reprinted in amended form. At stage three the Parliament decides whether to pass or reject the bill. If there is a division on whether the bill is passed, at least one quarter of the total number of MSPs must vote, whether for or against the bill or to abstain. Failing that, the division will be invalid and the bill will be treated as rejected. Once passed, the Presiding Officer will send the bill for Royal Assent unless a challenge to the competence of the bill is mounted as explained above.

The standing orders also make provision for member's bills, committee bills, budget bills, emergency bills, consolidation bills, statute law repeal bills and statute law revision bills. *Member's bills* are the equivalent in Scotland to private member's bills at Westminster, although the applicable procedural rules differ. All MSPs are entitled to introduce up to two member's bills in any one session, but to progress, the bill, within one month of being lodged with the clerk to the Parliament, must attract the support of at least 11 other MSPs. If it does so, it is printed and published, and thereafter follows the procedure prescribed for executive bills. *Committee bills* originate in proposals for legislation made by one of the parliamentary committees and set out in a report to the Parliament. If the Parliament agrees to the proposal, the committee convenor may instruct that a bill be drafted to implement the proposal, if this has not been done already, unless a member of the Scottish Executive undertakes to introduce an executive bill giving effect to the proposal instead. The subsequent stages of a committee bill, again, are exactly the same as those of an executive bill, except that at stage one the bill is referred directly to the Parliament for consideration of its general principles and a decision on whether these are agreed to. *Budget bills* are a special form of executive bill. Their three stages differ from the norm: at stage one, a budget bill is referred directly to the Parliament for consideration; stage two is taken by the Finance Committee; and stage three must be taken by the Parliament no sooner than 20 days, but no later than 30 days, following the bill's introduction. If stage three is not completed within thirty days of the bill's introduction, it will fail. *Emergency bills* are also a special form of executive bill, in relation to which the ordinary rules are disapplied and a fast-track procedure brought into play. The bill is referred directly to the Parliament for consideration of its general principles at stage one and stage two is taken by a Committee of the Whole Parliament. All three stages of the bill must be taken in the same day. The very first Act of the Scottish Parliament—the Mental Health (Public Safety and Appeals) (Scotland) Act 1999—was an emergency bill.

Chapter 9A of the standing orders makes provision in relation to private legislation. As at Westminster, private bills may be introduced by individuals, bodies corporate or unincorporated associations of persons in order to obtain for that person—"the promoter"—particular powers or benefits in excess of or in conflict with the general law. Following the introduction of a private bill and supporting documentation, a Private Bill Committee of up to five MSPs will be convened to consider the bill and report to the Parliament. If the bill is approved in principle, it is returned to the Committee for detailed scrutiny and consideration of objections and amendments. At the final stage, the Parliament decides whether or not the bill is passed.

COMMITTEES OF THE SCOTTISH PARLIAMENT

The rules concerning the committees of the Scottish Parliament are contained in Chapter 6 of the standing orders. The Parliament is required to establish and maintain, for the life of a Parliament, the following "mandatory" committees: Audit, Equal Opportunities, European and External Relations, Finance, Procedures, Public Petitions, Standards and Subordinate Legislation. The Parliament may also set up "subject" committees on the motion of any member. As we have seen, the committees of the Scottish Parliament play a key role in the legislative process in Scotland. In addition, they have the power to undertake inquiries on matters falling within their respective remits; examine the policy and administration of the Scottish Executive, including its financial administration; consider not only Scottish legislation but also legislation before the United Kingdom Parliament, European legislation or international agreements relating to matters falling within their remits; and to consider the need for law reform.

The Consultative Steering Group on the Scottish Parliament, which was set up prior to the establishment of the Parliament to make recommendations in relation to the procedural needs of the new body, saw the committees as one of the principal mechanisms for securing the values of openness, accessibility and responsiveness in the Scottish Parliament. To date they have proved to be an influential forum for public scrutiny of legislative proposals and executive policy, and they have undertaken a number of independent inquiries into matters of public importance.

PRIVILEGE IN THE SCOTTISH PARLIAMENT

The Scottish Parliament and its members do not enjoy the same range of privileges as exist at Westminster, and such privileges as they have find their source in the Scotland Act rather than ancient custom and practice.

The Scotland Act extends two aspects of the privilege of free speech to the Scottish Parliament, its members and officers. First, under section 41 of the Act, any statement made in proceedings of the Parliament and the publication under the authority of the Parliament of any statement is absolutely privileged in the law of defamation. Secondly, under section 42, certain proceedings of the Scottish Parliament—proceedings in relation to a bill or subordinate legislation—are shielded from criminal liability for contempt of court. A fair and accurate report of such proceedings, if made in good faith, is similarly protected.

Like members of the Westminster Parliament—but by virtue of section 85 of the Scotland Act rather than freedom from arrest and its associated privileges—MSPs are exempt from jury service. No immunity from civil or criminal arrest is extended to MSPs by the Scotland Act.

The privilege finding most echoes in the Scotland Act is that of exclusive cognisance of internal affairs. As it has been felt necessary at

Westminster to prevent outside interference, and specifically interference by the courts, with the proceedings of Parliament, so the Scotland Act makes provision rendering acts and decisions of the Parliament, its members and officers, and of members of the Scottish Executive, immune from legal challenge on the basis of alleged defects in their election, membership or appointment. A similar parallel is to be drawn between the inherent jurisdiction enjoyed by the Houses of Parliament at Westminster as the High Court of Parliament and the powers conferred on the Scottish Parliament in relation to witnesses, evidence and discipline. Sections 22 to 26 of the Scotland Act constitute a statutory statement of the extent to which the Scottish Parliament is to have an equivalent jurisdiction in these matters. As this implies, the jurisdiction of the ordinary courts is not wholly excluded in relation to the internal workings of the Scottish Parliament. For example, while by virtue of the Scotland Act it is a criminal offence to fail without reasonable excuse to comply with a notice from the Parliament compelling attendance or requiring the production of documents, these offences are triable in the ordinary courts rather than by the Parliament itself. Equally, the courts in Scotland have jurisdiction in relation to the registration of financial interests of members of the Scottish Parliament since provision for this is made not by way of standing orders but by way of subordinate legislation made under section 39 of the Scotland Act: *Whaley v Lord Watson of Invergowrie* (2000). But the courts do not have jurisdiction over the proceedings of the Scottish Parliament since these are regulated by standing orders contained in a resolution of the Scottish Parliament.

---

4. THE UNITED KINGDOM GOVERNMENT

INTRODUCTION

The functions of the state may be categorised as legislative, executive and judicial. The legislative function involves the making of laws of general application and the conferment of delegated legislative powers on other bodies. The judicial function involves the settlement of disputes of fact and law by the courts and other bodies vested with judicial powers. The executive function, broadly speaking, is what is left. It ranges from matters of high policy such as defence and foreign relations through to the day-to-day administration of public services.

Historically, the executive was identified with the person of the monarch and executive power with the royal prerogative. The vast majority of executive powers today derive from statute, but the prerogative remains an important source of executive power in certain areas of government. Most prerogative powers today are exercised by or on the advice of ministers, who are responsible to Parliament for the way in which they exercise these powers or the advice that they give. By the same token, the constitutional battles of the 17th century between Crown and Parliament, culminating in the revolution of 1688, settled that prerogative powers could be abolished, restricted or otherwise controlled by statute. Where a statute deals with the same subject-matter as a prerogative power, the former overrides the latter (*Attorney General v De Keyser's Royal Hotel* (1920)). However, *express* statutory words are needed if a prerogative power is to be abolished. As the House of Lords accepted in *Burmah Oil v Lord Advocate* (1964), the statute will otherwise merely apply until repealed, but once repealed the prerogative power will revive.

THE SOVEREIGN

The Queen is Head of State. In strict legal terms, the prerogatives of the Crown are vested in her, and a few prerogative powers, *e.g.* the conferment of certain honours, remain personal to the monarch. Note, however, that in modern usage "the Crown" is for practical purposes synonymous with "central government", and it is ministers of the Crown who exercise prerogative powers or advise on their exercise. Even the term "advise" is misleading because, by convention, the Sovereign's freedom of action is very limited.

Essentially, therefore, the executive role of the Sovereign is dignified rather than effective. Yet it has been said that the Sovereign has three rights—the right to be consulted, the right to encourage and the right to warn. Moreover, there may be circumstances in which the constitutional role of the Sovereign *could* assume an effective dimension.

Hung Parliaments and the prerogatives of appointment and dissolution

The Sovereign appoints a Prime Minister in an exercise of the prerogative. Modern politics, coupled with the constraints of convention, mean that the prerogative of appointment will fasten on the person who is best able to command the confidence of the Commons—the leader of the party having an overall majority of seats in the House. General elections usually produce such majorities but, in the event of a hung Parliament, what should happen may be less clear.

In the election of December 1923, the Prime Minister, Mr Baldwin, lost his overall majority in the Commons, although his was still the largest party. He continued in office and waited to meet Parliament, as he was entitled to do. Baldwin was then defeated in the vote on the King's Speech—a matter of confidence—and at that point resigned, because plainly he was unable to command the confidence of the Commons. The King appointed Mr MacDonald as Prime Minister. There was no fresh election and no need of one; and the choice of MacDonald involved no exercise of discretion on the King's part. It was dictated by the political circumstances: coalition under Baldwin being impossible, MacDonald was best placed to command the confidence of the Commons as the head of a minority government.

In the election of 1929, Mr Baldwin lost his majority again. This time his party was no longer even the largest party in the Commons, although no other party had an overall majority either. Baldwin resigned immediately: the factors which had prevented him leading a coalition government or relying on support from other parties in 1923 were still present. Again, the King sent for Mr MacDonald and, again, no royal discretion was involved in that choice.

However, the Prime Minister in this situation is not obliged to resign immediately. If the possibility of coalition exists, the Prime Minister may explore it. So in February 1974, Mr Heath did not resign until four days after the election, during which time he pursued—unsuccessfully—the prospect of a coalition Cabinet containing Liberal MPs. Labour was the largest party by five seats and was prepared to form a government with no help from other parties even though it lacked an overall majority. The Queen duly sent for Mr Wilson.

None of these hung Parliaments required recourse to the Sovereign in anything but a formal sense. But there are no rules to govern these situations, and the precedents themselves only provide guidance. Thus hung Parliaments *might* produce situations in which the Sovereign would have to act without, or even in the face of, ministerial advice. For example, a minority administration is formed but is shortly defeated on a motion of no-confidence, or a coalition government is formed but collapses within weeks of the election. The Prime Minister concludes that the newly-elected Parliament is unworkable, because incapable of sustaining a government in office, and advises the Queen to dissolve Parliament a second time so that a second election may be held. How should the Queen respond?

In 1951, the King's Private Secretary set out the principles governing (in his view) the Sovereign's right to refuse a second dissolution:

> "The Sovereign could properly refuse a dissolution if satisfied that a) the existing Parliament was still vital, viable and capable of doing its job; b) a general election would be detrimental to the national economy; c) he could rely on finding another Prime Minister who could carry on his government for a reasonable period with a working majority."

Thus, had Mr Heath not resigned in 1974 but requested a second dissolution, the Queen would have been entitled to refuse because an alternative administration to Mr Heath's was available.

The position may differ, however, if the second dissolution is requested not by the Prime Minister who requested the first, but by his successor in a hung Parliament. In 1974, Mr Wilson assumed that a dissolution was his for the asking at any time, with or without defeat on a motion of confidence. In the volatile circumstances of 1974, he was probably right, and he did go to the country again in October 1974. However, Mr Wilson might not have been right if the Conservatives and Liberals had managed in the meantime to agree on some form of coalition government, because then an administration could have been formed from the existing Parliament.

In short, any theory of "automatic dissolution" at the request of the Prime Minister must be regarded as misconceived. It is unlikely that the role of the Sovereign will be anything more than formal, even in cases of difficulty. There should be no reason to refuse a request for a dissolution and no need for royal discretion in the choice of Prime Minister. However, the prerogatives of the Crown in this area provide a "safety valve" should it appear that politicians are abusing the system, and the fact that the powers exist may deter such abuse. Moreover, there are examples of exercise of the prerogatives in response to perceived abuse. In 1926, the minority Liberal Prime Minister in Canada requested a dissolution from the Sovereign's representative, the Governor-General. The Governor-General believed that the Conservative leader could form a government having majority support in the existing Parliament, and refused. The Prime Minister resigned and the Governor-General appointed the Conservative leader in his place. Days later, the new government was defeated on a motion of confidence, leading to the dissolution which had been denied to its Liberal predecessor. In the general election that followed, the Liberals were returned with a convincing majority. This illustrates that the Sovereign should not seek personally to exercise her legal powers in anything but extreme circumstances. It does not, however, prove that the personal exercise of the prerogatives of appointment and dissolution , will always be unconstitutional.

The prerogative of dismissal

As the Sovereign's effective power to appoint a Prime Minister is reduced almost to nothing by convention, so too is the Sovereign's power to dismiss a Prime Minister. Indeed in *Adegbenro v Akintola* (1964), Lord Radcliffe stated that the exercise of the "Sovereign's right of removal ... is not regarded as being within the scope of practical politics".

Yet the right of removal has been exercised in recent times. In 1975, Australia was governed by a Labour administration under Mr Whitlam, but the Opposition had a majority of seats in the Australian Senate. The Senate refused to pass money bills authorising government expenditure, which led to a rapid depletion in the funds available to maintain public services. Mr Whitlam requested the Governor-General to dissolve the Senate. The Governor-General was only prepared to grant a full dissolution so that there could be a general election. When Mr Whitlam refused to change his advice, the Governor-General dismissed him and his government and appointed Mr Fraser, the Opposition leader, in his place, on condition that he would guarantee supply and advise a dissolution and general election. In the event, Mr Fraser won the election.

Was this situation so extreme as to justify the exercise of the prerogative of dismissal? Arguably, the Sovereign should only exercise her prerogatives personally and without advice where necessary to safeguard the parliamentary and democratic basis of the constitution (e.g. where a government fails to seek a dissolution of Parliament after five years have expired since the last election). Beyond that, the legitimacy of the monarchy rests upon political neutrality on the part of the Sovereign, and the appearance of neutrality would be gravely undermined were the Sovereign to intervene in anything other than a constitutional crisis, where it is more or less clear that the "safety valve" must be pressed into service.

CENTRAL GOVERNMENT

The Prime Minister

The Prime Minister is a creature of constitutional convention. There is hardly any legal underpinning to the office and only cursory recognition of the office in statute. It is rare for statutes to confer powers on the Prime Minister. His powers flow, essentially, from the fact of being in charge, and so long as the Prime Minister retains the confidence of his Cabinet and party, these powers are extensive. For example, it is the Prime Minister who generally advises the Queen on the exercise of important prerogatives of the Crown, and it is the Prime Minister who controls the machinery of central government. These powers are reinforced by the convention of collective ministerial responsibility, whereby all government ministers are bound to defend and promote government policy, however that may be arrived at.

The Deputy Prime Minister

Formerly there was doubt as to the existence of this office. The objection was that, by nominating a deputy, the Prime Minister was pre-empting the royal prerogative of appointment by setting out a preferred line of succession. This must now be regarded as irrelevant. Labour governments have tended to include a Deputy Prime Minister to underscore the status of the elected deputy leader of the party. The deputy leadership of the Conservative party, by contrast, is in the gift of the leader, who may choose to appoint a Deputy Prime Minister. Certainly the Prime Minister is not bound to appoint a deputy, but there are no longer any constitutional difficulties if he chooses to do so, and there may be good political and administrative reasons for the appointment.

Ministers of the Crown

Section 8(1) of the Ministers of the Crown Act 1975 defines a minister as "the holder of any office in Her Majesty's Government in the United Kingdom". Ministers are appointed to their office by the Queen on the advice of the Prime Minister.

We may distinguish between Cabinet ministers, usually designated Secretaries of State, who have overall responsibility for particular departments, and departmental ministers of state, who share in the administration of a department and who may have specific portfolios. Parliamentary private secretaries are appointed to assist in a department's parliamentary work, but are not ministers.

By convention, ministers must be members of the House of Commons or the House of Lords. Section 2 of the House of Commons Disqualification Act 1975 provides that no more than 95 ministers may sit and vote in the Commons. Schedule 1 to the Ministerial and Other Salaries Act 1975 places limits on the total number of ministerial salaries payable at any one time. These provisions are practical limitations on the Prime Minister's power of patronage, but there is no legal limit on the number of ministers that the Crown may appoint, provided that the excess are members of the House of Lords and/or unpaid. Peers as ministers are a necessary consequence of the statutory provisions, and it is not uncommon for a political ally of the Prime Minister to be elevated to high office through the conferment of a life peerage.

The Law Officers of the Crown are also members of the United Kingdom government. For England and Wales, they are the Attorney-General and the Solicitor-General, and they are always drawn from the House of Commons. The Lord Advocate and the Solicitor-General for Scotland used likewise to be members of the United Kingdom Government, but by virtue of section 48 of the Scotland Act they are now members of the Scottish Executive. This necessitated the appointment of a new Scottish Law Officer in the United Kingdom government, a need met by the provision in section 87 of the Scotland Act for the office of Advocate General for Scotland.

The Cabinet

Like the Prime Minister, the Cabinet is a creature of convention—there are no legal rules governing its composition, functions or procedure, although the Ministerial and Other Salaries Act 1975 restricts the number of salaried Cabinet posts to 20, apart from the Prime Minister and Lord Chancellor.

The Cabinet emerged and developed in the late 18th century. In the 19th century, when government was relatively small, it was the engine-room of government; and it has been likened to the board of directors of a company. Collectively and in private, the Cabinet discussed and decided on government policy, resolved disputes between departments and provided general oversight and co-ordination. This traditional model of

Cabinet government was bound together by conventions relating to the confidentiality of Cabinet discussions and collective responsibility for government policy. If a Cabinet minister felt unable to support agreed policy, convention required him to resign.

In the 20th century, however, this traditional model came under some strain. In 1963, Richard Crossman argued that the Cabinet had become a dignified rather than effective institution; and in 1983, the former Cabinet Secretary Lord Hunt said that "we are imposing more and more on a system of collective decision-taking that was designed for quite a different era." Government has grown immensely in volume, intensity and complexity, yet the Cabinet is still the same size and still meets only once a week. Efforts have been made to improve the capacity of the Cabinet to cope with modern demands, notably in establishing the Cabinet Office after World War One; and, since World War Two, in delegating much Cabinet business to Cabinet committees. Now, the Ministerial Code of Conduct states that issues should so far as possible be settled in committee, and only brought to Cabinet proper where agreement is impossible.

These developments contributed to a dispersal of power away from the Cabinet. From being the effective heart of the government machine in the 19th century, the Cabinet today considers few policy and legislative initiatives, and even those matters which are referred to Cabinet go there in most cases only for rubber-stamping rather than proper consideration and collective commitment. A further consequence in the decline of traditional Cabinet government, some argue, is an increase in the powers of the Prime Minister. Crossman suggested that the institutional mechanisms and conventions which once served a collective, collegiate body had come to serve the Prime Minister instead. Thus the Cabinet Office was in reality the Prime Minister's Office, and collective responsibility, which had once meant the responsibility of a group of equal colleagues for decisions taken collectively, had come to mean "collective obedience to the will of the man at the apex of power". More recently, the inquiry under Lord Butler into the use made of intelligence on weapons of mass destruction in Iraq suggested that the "informality" of much of the present government's decision making, and relative lack of use of established Cabinet committee machinery, reduced the scope for informed collective political judgment. Yet however powerful the Prime Minister may be, that power is ultimately conditional upon the support of the Cabinet (as the example of Mrs Thatcher amply illustrates). This is true even when the government is supported by a healthy Commons majority, and truer still when its majority is fragile.

Scottish representation in the United Kingdom Government
With the transfer of functions from the United Kingdom government to the Scottish Executive on July 1, 1999, the former Scottish Office was re-named the Scotland Office and the number of ministers working within it,

including the Secretary of State for Scotland, was reduced to two (although the Advocate General for Scotland is also attached to the Scotland Office).

The Secretary of State for Scotland remains a member of the United Kingdom Cabinet and has certain important functions under the Scotland Act, not least of which is his function of paying grants into the Scottish Consolidated Fund and managing other financial transactions arising out of devolution. In addition, the fact that much that is of concern to Scotland remains reserved to Westminster ensures a continuing role for the Secretary of State. He is also seen as having a role to play in fostering the devolution settlement, liaising between the United Kingdom and Scottish tiers of government and promoting co-operation between the two Parliaments.

Perhaps the powers of the Secretary of State with the greatest potential significance are his powers to intervene in certain circumstances in relation to Scottish legislation and acts of the Scottish Executive. In the first case, after a bill has been passed by the Scottish Parliament, a four-week delay must normally be observed before it can be sent for Royal Assent. During that time, the Secretary of State may, under section 35 of the Scotland Act, make an order prohibiting the submission of the bill for Royal Assent if it contains provisions which he has reasonable grounds to believe would be incompatible with any international obligations of the United Kingdom or with the interests of defence or national security, or which modify the law as it applies to matters reserved to Westminster in a way which he has reasonable grounds to believe would have an adverse effect on the operation of the law as it applies to reserved matters. This power may be used whether or not it is claimed that the provisions of the bill fall outwith the legislative competence of the Scottish Parliament. In the second case, the Secretary of State may, under section 58 of the Scotland Act, make an order directing the Scottish Executive not to take action where he has reasonable grounds to believe that such action would be incompatible with any international obligations of the United Kingdom. By the same token, he may require the Scottish Executive to act where he has reasonable grounds to believe that such action is necessary to give effect to such obligations. Section 58 also entitles the Secretary of State to intervene in the making of subordinate legislation by the Scottish Executive.

We have seen that, with the devolution to Scotland of most of the issues falling within the competence of the Lord Advocate and Solicitor-General for Scotland, it was considered appropriate that both should cease to be ministers in the United Kingdom Government and become members of the Scottish Executive. But the United Kingdom Government continues to need advice from time to time on matters of Scots law and advice and representation on "devolution issues". For this reason, the Scotland Act created a new ministerial office of Advocate General for Scotland. Apart from her advisory and representative role, the Advocate General also has power under section 33 of the Scotland Act (in common with the Lord Advocate and Attorney General for England and Wales) to refer to the Privy Council the question of whether a bill passed by the Scottish Parliament is outwith the legislative competence of the Parliament.

The government machine

The theory of the British constitution frequently fails to reflect actual constitutional practice, and this is perhaps especially true in relation to the theory and practice of the business of government. A great deal of constitutional doctrine is founded upon a notion of the constitution in which governmental tasks are shared out between a number of government departments, headed by Cabinet ministers and run by a team of professional civil servants. The ministerial bosses are more or less able to supervise the workings of their respective departments and so to take responsibility for them in Parliament. Yet this portrait of constitutional practice is a misleading one, not least because, following fundamental reform of the structure of the civil service, much of the business of government is in fact conducted at some distance from the ministerial core.

These reforms of the government machine, stemming from concerns about the size, cost and inefficiency of the civil service, initially took the form of downsizing and pay restraints. But in 1988, the report *Improving Management in Government: The Next Steps* recommended the complete separation of policy-making functions from service-delivery functions. The latter, covering an estimated 95 per cent of civil service activity, would be devolved to *executive agencies* instead of being undertaken by traditional Whitehall departments. Departments were therefore required to review their activities and assess their suitability for hiving off to agencies. The rigour of the procedure intensified in 1991 with the introduction of "market testing". This requires departments to look at particular functions and ask whether that function can be abolished; if not, whether it can be privatised; if not, whether it can be contracted out to a private company; if not, whether it can be hived off to an agency. Only if the answer to all of these questions is "no" should things stay as they are.

Nearly 200 executive agencies have been established and, as the 1988 report predicted, over 90 per cent of civil servants now work for agencies. Each agency operates within the terms of a framework document, which sets out the respective responsibilities of the relevant minister and agency chief executive, performance targets (including strict financial targets and spending limits) and other operating arrangements. Initially, the chief executive answered to the minister for his agency's performance in implementing the policies settled by the minister; the minister, in turn, answered to Parliament for the agency's work—at least in theory. Now, the accountability of agencies to Parliament is more direct. Written questions are referred, where appropriate, to agency chief executives, who routinely appear before select committees to answer for their operational effectiveness.

Executive agencies are only one aspect of what is often termed "New Public Management" or the "marketisation" of the state. The dynamic behind the reforms is a belief that governmental efficiency can be improved by re-modelling government in a way which mimics the private sector and the efficient practices and disciplines of the free market. Other products of this dynamic are the privatisation of nationalised industries, the contracting out to private companies of public functions and the increasing co-option of private enterprise into the business of providing public services through "public/private partnerships". Nor have the reforms taken place only on the "supply side". In a genuine market, consumers have a part to play. Thus the Citizen's Charter initiative was launched in 1991, to specify what the government's "customers" are entitled to expect from public services and to provide mechanisms for redress should those expectations be disappointed.

Efficiency in government is an important objective. But it is argued that efficiency cannot be measured in terms of cost-cutting alone and that this objective must be balanced against the objective of providing high quality public services. Also, concern has been expressed that the "marketising" of the state has created a tension between old-fashioned administrative relationships based on the ethos of public service, and contractual or quasi-contractual relationships based on the profit motive and pursuit of efficiency. Whatever the merits or demerits of the marketising of the state, it is here to stay. Far from rejecting it, the new Labour government elected in 1997 enthusiastically endorsed New Public Management in all its forms. Yet there remain important questions, not least about whether the re-packaging of governmental power has been accompanied by the creation of adequate avenues of accountability.

ACCOUNTABILITY

Accountability, an obligation resting on those who exercise power over others, has two aspects. The *explanatory* aspect involves justifying and explaining why certain policies were pursued and certain decisions taken. The *amendatory* aspect involves accepting blame when things go wrong and ensuring that mistakes are rectified. Accountability is important for two reasons. First, government is not infallible. Accountability should reduce the risks associated with governmental fallibility, for if government bodies feel obliged to justify their decisions and answer for their mistakes, they are more likely to think things through properly and avoid making mistakes in the first place. Secondly, although one may disagree with a government and its policies, it is easier to accept its decisions if one is confident that it takes care in making its decisions, that it acts in good faith and is willing to be held to account. Thus accountability is a form of "institutional morality" in a liberal democracy: it is conducive to cohesion.

According to traditional constitutional theory, the main avenue of accountability is political—the responsibility of ministers to Parliament for policy choices and the quality of administration. In keeping with this traditional view, civil servants bear no constitutional responsibility for departmental errors: the minister must answer for them. It is one of Parliament's key constitutional functions to scrutinise and check the executive, and to enforce ministers' obligation to explain and justify departmental acts and decisions. When a minister cannot satisfactorily account for something that took place within his department, then the Commons may withdraw its confidence from the minister on a motion of censure, forcing the minister to resign. The minister might pre-empt this by resigning anyway. Similarly, where the government as a whole comes under attack for its policies and loses the confidence of the Commons, the government collectively is obliged to resign. This doctrine is the basis of the traditional convention of ministerial responsibility.

There are some examples of resignations apparently in accordance with the convention, notably that of Sir Thomas Dugdale over the Crichel Down Affair in 1954, and, in 1982, those of the Foreign Secretary, Lord Carrington, and two Foreign Office ministers because of failure to predict Argentine intentions prior to the Falklands War. But the great majority of ministerial resignations have less to do with proven incompetence or error than other factors, such as personal or financial scandal. It is therefore argued that reliance on the convention of ministerial responsibility to Parliament as the primary mechanism of accountability is worthless, because the convention is no longer operative. This is partly because the Commons itself no longer works in a way which would enable it to withdraw its confidence from failing ministers. As Finer said:

> "[M]ost charges never reach the stage of individualisation at all: they are stifled under the blanket of party solidarity. Whether a minister is forced to resign depends on three factors: on himself, his Prime Minister and his party. For a resignation to occur, all three factors have to be just so, the minister compliant, the Prime Minister firm, the party clamorous. This conjuncture is rare."

But a convention which stipulates loss of office as a penalty seems unrealistic and unfair today. The growth of government means that individual ministers cannot be expected anymore to know about everything that takes place within their departments. Unless the minister is personally at fault, should he be expected to resign? After the Crichel Down Affair, the Home Secretary, Sir David Maxwell-Fyfe, appeared to suggest that he should not:

> "In the case where there is an explicit order by a minister, the minister must protect the civil servant who has carried out the order. Equally, where a civil servant acts properly in accordance with the policy laid down by the minister, the minister must protect and defend him. Where an official makes a mistake … but not on an

> important issue of policy ... the minister acknowledges the mistake and ... states that he will take corrective action within his department. [But] where action has been taken by a civil servant of which the minister disapproves and has no prior knowledge ... [he] is not bound to defend [the civil servant]."

There are indications that such an approach is taken in practice. Thus in 1983, following the mass breakout of IRA prisoners from the Maze Prison, the Secretary of State for Northern Ireland refused to accept any constitutional obligation to resign in the absence of proven culpability on his part (which he denied) as distinct from the culpability of civil servants in the Northern Ireland Office: his responsibility for policy had to be distinguished from his responsibility for mere administration. This policy/administration distinction has resurfaced in the light of the "marketising" of the state. It has been asserted that while "the minister is properly accountable for the policies which he settles ... those who have agreed to provide the services are quite properly responsible for their provision."

But the controversy over the management of the Prison Service in 1995, during which the Home Secretary sacked the agency's chief executive, illustrates the strains in the policy/administration distinction. The Home Secretary, when pressed in the Commons to resign over the mismanagement of the Prison Service, argued that this was the province of the chief executive. Yet the chief executive stated publicly that he had never been able to get to grips with improving management because of constant interference in administration by the Home Office. More importantly, the distinction is only valid if ministers remember that, even if they are no longer under an obligation to resign unless personally at fault for errors of policy, they do retain an obligation to *account* to Parliament, even in respect of matters for which responsibility has been delegated. Sir David Maxwell-Fyfe stressed this:

> "[The minister alone] remains constitutionally responsible to Parliament for the fact that something has gone wrong, and he alone can tell Parliament what has occurred and render an account of his stewardship."

But it is far from clear that the supposedly unimpaired duty to account to Parliament—to provide Parliament with information, to explain and to justify—is being honoured in practice.

5. THE GOVERNMENT OF SCOTLAND

THE SCOTTISH EXECUTIVE AND SCOTTISH ADMINISTRATION

While "executive" functions range from matters of high government policy through to the more mundane, day to day running of public services, the term "the Scottish Executive" has a specific, and narrower, meaning under the Scotland Act. It refers to the core of Scottish Government—the First Minister, the Scottish Ministers and the Law Officers. The Scottish Executive in this sense is the central element of the wider "Scottish Administration", which also includes junior Scottish Ministers, non-ministerial office-holders such as the Keeper of the Registers of Scotland, and civil servants who are appointed to the staff of the Scottish Administration.

This statutory definition should not, of course, blind one to the fact that the United Kingdom Government continues to exercise extensive executive powers in relation to Scotland. Moreover, as at the United Kingdom level, when one looks beyond the Scottish Executive in the technical, narrow sense, one perceives the much wider range of public authorities charged with the exercise of executive authority over the people of Scotland.

The First Minister

We have seen that, at the United Kingdom level, there are few legal rules governing the selection and appointment of the Prime Minister, although the constitutional conventions on the subject are well-settled. The conventional model of parliamentary government has largely been replicated, in statutory form, in the Scotland Act. Like the Prime Minister, then, the First Minister is appointed by the Queen from among the members of the Scottish Parliament; and like the Prime Minister, he holds office at Her Majesty's pleasure. He may at any time resign his office, and under section 45 of the Scotland Act he must do so if the Parliament resolves that the Scottish Executive no longer enjoys the confidence of the Parliament.

Although the Queen carries out the formal task of appointment, she will act on the nomination, communicated to her by the Presiding Officer, of the Parliament itself. The Parliament must make its nomination within 28 days of a Scottish general election, the resignation of the incumbent First Minister, the office of the First Minister falling vacant for a reason other than resignation, or the First Minister ceasing to be an MSP otherwise than by reason of the dissolution of the Scottish Parliament. Chapter 4 of the standing orders of the Scottish Parliament makes further provision in relation to the process for nominating a member for appointment as First Minister. If no candidate is successful in securing the Parliament's nomination, the Presiding Officer must arrange for another selection process to take place as soon as possible and in any case within 28 days of the triggering event. If that period expires without a nomination being made, the Scotland Act obliges the Presiding Officer to propose a date for the holding of an extraordinary general election. The results of that election may produce a party balance in the Scottish Parliament more favourable to the nomination of one of its number to be First Minister.

The Scottish Ministers

Once the First Minister has been appointed, it falls to him under section 47 of the Scotland Act to appoint the other members of the Scottish Executive and the junior Scottish Ministers. Like the First Minister, the Scottish Ministers must be members of the Scottish Parliament and their appointment must meet with the formal approval of the Queen. The First Minister may not seek the Queen's approval for any ministerial appointment without the agreement of the Parliament as signified in accordance with standing orders. There is nothing in the Scotland Act or elsewhere to dictate to the First Minister how many ministers he may appoint or what their individual portfolios should be: the First Minister apart, the only "named" members of the Scottish Executive are the Lord Advocate and the Solicitor General for Scotland. Once appointed, the Scottish Ministers hold office at Her Majesty's pleasure, which is to say that they are, in theory, dismissable by the Queen. They may in any case be removed from office at any time by the First Minister. A minister may resign his office at any time and must do so if the Parliament passes a vote of no confidence in the Scottish Executive.

Junior Scottish Ministers

Junior Scottish Ministers are appointed by the First Minister under section 49 of the Scotland Act, again with the approval of the Queen and the agreement of the Parliament. Their task is to assist the Scottish Ministers in the exercise of their functions, and their tenure of office is on the same terms as that of the Scottish Ministers proper.

The Law Officers for Scotland

The offices of Lord Advocate and Solicitor General for Scotland can both boast a long historical pedigree. Prior to devolution, they were offices in the government of the United Kingdom, carrying substantial ministerial responsibilities. They represented the Crown before the Scottish courts, advised the government on issues of Scots law, controlled the system of public prosecutions in Scotland and took charge of the drafting of bills applying to Scotland. Many of the functions relating to law reform and the machinery of justice, which for England and Wales are performed by the Lord Chancellor, were in Scotland vested in the Lord Advocate. Since the devolution of competence over Scots criminal law and procedure, the criminal justice system and the Scottish courts encompassed most of the responsibilities of the Scottish Law Officers, however, it was felt appropriate that they should cease to be ministers of the Crown in the government of the United Kingdom and instead become members of the Scottish Executive. This was duly provided for by the Scotland Act, although the position of the Law Officers remains special and distinct from that of their Scottish ministerial colleagues in a number of respects.

First, it is now for the First Minister, acting under section 48 of the Scotland Act, to recommend to the Queen the appointment of a person as Lord Advocate or Solicitor General (formerly, the Queen made the appointments on the advice of the Prime Minister). Neither the Lord Advocate nor the Solicitor General need be a member of the Scottish Parliament. As with the appointment of the Scottish Ministers and junior Scottish Ministers, however, the First Minister must secure the Parliament's agreement before he can send forward his nominations. It should be noted that, with the Law Officers, the Queen actually makes the appointment; she does not, as with the Scottish Ministers, merely approve the choice of the First Minister. Moreover, once appointed, the Law Officers cannot be removed from office by the First Minister. Only the Queen may do this, on the recommendation of the First Minister and with the agreement of the Scottish Parliament. This greater security of tenure reflects the greater constitutional significance of the Law Officers' role in the administration of justice in Scotland and the correspondingly greater need for a degree of independence on their part. The independence of the Lord Advocate is further secured by a number of provisions scattered throughout the Scotland Act, including section 29 (which excludes the competence of the Scottish Parliament to legislate in such a way as to remove the Lord Advocate from his position as head of the systems of criminal prosecution and investigation of deaths) and section 48(5) (which states that "any decision of the Lord Advocate in his capacity as head of the systems of criminal prosecution and investigation of deaths in Scotland shall continue to be taken by him independently of any other person").

SOURCES OF EXECUTIVE POWER

At the United Kingdom level, there are two basic sources of executive power: statute, and the royal prerogative. But the Scottish Executive, being a creation of statute, has no inherent powers and must locate the source of all its authority in legislation—namely, the Scotland Act.

Scottish legislation

Section 52 of the Scotland Act provides for the conferment of statutory functions on the Scottish Ministers, and in time, the majority of the functions of the Scottish Executive will find their source in Acts of the Scottish Parliament and Scottish statutory instruments. In reserved areas, however, Acts of the Westminster Parliament may confer functions on the Scottish Ministers. And in the meantime, many of the executive powers exercised by the Scottish Ministers are in fact founded in United Kingdom legislation or (to a lesser extent) the prerogative. The logic of devolution demanded not only that legislative competence over devolved matters be transferred from Westminster to the Scottish Parliament but also that executive competence over these matters (and others) be transferred from ministers in the United Kingdom Government to the Scottish Ministers.

Transferred ministerial functions

The transfer of ministerial functions is provided for by section 53 of the Scotland Act, which states that so far as a statutory function conferred on a minister of the Crown is exercisable within devolved competence, it shall instead be exercisable by the Scottish Ministers. The same is true of prerogative functions. The concept of "devolved competence" is defined by reference to the definition of legislative competence contained in section 29 of the Scotland Act. Generally speaking, then, it will be outwith the competence of the Scottish Executive to act in breach of the Convention rights or European Community law, or to act in the sphere of reserved matters. It is important to note, however, that the limits of "devolved competence" are extended by the conferment on the Scottish Executive of powers which do not fall within the Scottish Parliament's legislative competence, and by provision for various degrees of co-operation and consultation in governmental decision making between the Scottish Executive and the United Kingdom Government. This is because section 63 of the Scotland Act provides for the transfer of *additional* functions, exercisable by a minister of the Crown in or as regards Scotland, to the Scottish Ministers. The point to remember here is that, although the subject matter of such functions does not fall within the scope of "devolved competence" in the sense that the Scottish Parliament would be able to legislate on them, it is nevertheless deemed appropriate that the exercise of certain powers in areas reserved to Westminster be entrusted to the Scottish Ministers, or that the Scottish Ministers be involved in their exercise to some lesser extent. Pursuant to section 63, therefore, the Queen may by Order in Council provide for specified functions to be exercised by the Scottish Ministers instead of by a minister of the Crown; by the Scottish Ministers concurrently with a minister of the Crown; or by a minister of the Crown only with the agreement of, or after consultation with, the Scottish Ministers. Conversely, under section 56 of the Scotland Act, a number of statutory powers involving funding or grant-making powers continue, despite the provision for automatic transfer of functions falling within devolved competence, to be exercisable by ministers of the Crown as well as by the Scottish Ministers. The list of such "shared powers" may be modified by subordinate legislation.

Functions in relation to Community law and Convention rights

The Scotland Act also makes provision for executive functions in relation to Community law and the Convention rights. As to the first of these, compatibility with Community law is, by virtue of section 54 as reinforced by section 57(2) of the Scotland Act, a condition of the legality of the acts of members of the Scottish Executive as much as it is a condition of the validity of Scottish legislation. However, while general competence in relation to foreign affairs is reserved by Schedule 5 to Westminster, "observing and implementing ... obligations under Community law" are expressly exempted from the scope of that reservation. Two consequences follow from this. First, the Scottish Parliament has a degree of positive competence as regards the implementation in Scotland of Community obligations. Secondly, so far as the power conferred on ministers of the Crown by section 2(2) of the European Communities Act 1972 (to implement or give effect to the obligations of the United Kingdom arising under Community law) is exercisable within devolved competence, it is by virtue of section 53 of the Scotland Act exercisable in or as regards Scotland by the Scottish Ministers.

This seems to set up a reasonably straightforward division of labour in Community matters between the United Kingdom government and Scottish Executive. But it is complicated somewhat by the terms of section 57 of the Scotland Act, which states that despite the transfer under section 53 to the Scottish Ministers of functions concerning the implementation of Community obligations in Scotland, "any function of a minister of the Crown in relation to any matter shall continue to be exercisable by him as regards Scotland for the purposes specified in section 2(2) of the European Communities Act 1972." This suggests that even where the Scottish Ministers have acted to implement their understanding of a Community obligation in Scotland, a United Kingdom minister may nonetheless make different (and overriding) provision. But if so, it would seem to follow that where the Scottish Ministers have failed to act, or even where they have acted on a mistaken view of Community law, any liability for breach of Community law must be brought home to the United Kingdom Government if they in turn fail to exercise the overarching power reserved to them by section 57(1).

Likewise, members of the Scottish Executive cannot lawfully act (or fail to act) in a manner incompatible with the Convention rights. Here there is less complexity: the prohibition is absolute in its terms, except so far as it is qualified by section 57(3) in relation to acts of the Lord Advocate in prosecuting any offence or in his capacity as head of the systems of criminal prosecution and investigation of deaths which "because of subsection (2) to section 6 of the Human Rights Act 1998 is not unlawful under subsection (1) of that section". Section 6 of the Human Rights Act makes it unlawful for a "public authority" to act in a manner inconsistent with the Convention rights unless (subsection (2)) the authority is unable to act in any other way because of the terms of the legislation pursuant to which it is acting. In that event, the public authority—or, for the purposes of section 57(3), the Lord Advocate—has a defence and the only remedy left the aggrieved individual is a "declaration of incompatibility" under section 4 of the Human Rights Act. However, it must first be shown that the relevant legislation truly cannot be read and given effect in a manner compatible with the Convention rights. In that sense, the onus is on all public authorities, including the Lord Advocate, to strive, so far as possible, to read and give effect to enabling legislation in a Convention-proofed way. Only if that cannot be done will the "defence" under section 6(2) come into play. And it should be pointed out that the limitation of the terms of section 57(3) of the Scotland Act to certain acts of the Lord Advocate suggests that the other members of the Scottish Executive (and indeed the Lord Advocate himself so far as any of his functions are not caught by section 57(3)) cannot take the benefit of the section 6(2) defence in any circumstances but are, together with the Scottish Parliament, subject to an absolute duty to comply with the Convention rights.

THE CIVIL SERVICE

Under section 30 and Schedule 5 of the Scotland Act, the civil service of the United Kingdom is a matter reserved to Westminster. Thus the staff of the Scottish Administration are, as before devolution, members of the Home Civil Service rather than members of a distinctively Scottish civil service. As before, they hold office under the Crown on terms and conditions determined in accordance with the Civil Service Management Code in common with their colleagues elsewhere in the United Kingdom. Within this framework, however, it is for the Scottish Ministers to appoint members of the staff of the Scottish Administration, and the payment of their salaries, pensions and allowances is chargeable on the Scottish Consolidated Fund.

SCOTTISH PUBLIC AUTHORITIES

We have seen that, at the United Kingdom level of government, much of the day-to-day business of government is conducted by authorities and agencies at arm's length from the central governmental core. So too in Scotland, beyond the Scottish Executive and Scottish Administration as defined above, there are a great many public authorities charged with greater or lesser amounts of administrative or executive authority. It should be noted that, strictly speaking, the term "Scottish public authorities" has a special meaning under the Scotland Act, which defines them in section 126 to include only those public bodies, public offices or holders of such offices whose functions are exercisable in or as regards Scotland. But if the term is understood in a wider and generic sense, it might be said that public authorities in Scotland, local authorities and central executive departments aside, fall into four categories.

First, there are bodies which are wholly devolved in the sense that their functions fall within the legislative competence of the Scottish Parliament (which may therefore legislate to change their functions, alter their structure or even wind them up and create new ones) and in the sense that the Scottish Executive has inherited the powers of the United Kingdom government in relation to them. They include certain nationalised industries, public corporations, tribunals and health authorities, and a tranche of executive and advisory non-departmental public bodies such as Scottish Enterprise, the Scottish Environmental Protection Agency, the Scottish Legal Aid Board and the Scottish Law Commission.

Then there are bodies which might be described as hybrid in various senses. Some exercise functions in both devolved and reserved spheres; others have functions falling wholly within the scope of devolved competence but do not confine their activities to Scotland; and others still are hybrid in both senses, having a mixture of reserved and devolved functions exercisable both in and beyond Scotland. The treatment of such bodies in the Scotland Act is two-fold. On the one hand, it makes special provision in sections 88 to 90 for bodies designated as "cross-border public authorities" which exercise functions falling within devolved competence, in or as regards Scotland, but which have "other functions" relating to reserved matters, to matters exercisable other than in Scotland, or both. These include the British Tourist Authority, the National Consumer Council and the National Criminal Intelligence Service. No special provision is made for bodies not designated as cross-border public authorities, but there are scattered references throughout the Scotland Act to public authorities with "mixed functions". While in terms of paragraph 1 of Part III of Schedule 5 to the Scotland Act, such bodies are not reserved as such, their position differs in certain important respects from that of truly devolved bodies. In particular, the Scottish Parliament cannot amend or abolish such functions of a mixed body as do not fall within its legislative competence, and the power to establish, maintain or abolish Scottish public authorities having mixed functions is not exclusive to the Scottish Ministers but is shared and exercisable jointly with ministers of the Crown.

Lastly, there are bodies, such as the BBC, which are reserved in the sense that they operate on a United Kingdom or Great Britain basis and entirely in relation to reserved matters. As such, they remain subject to the supervision and control of Westminster and Whitehall. Their functions are, however, of interest to Scotland, and for that reason certain provision is made to ensure that regard is had to the Scottish dimension to their activities.

CONCORDATS

At both the legislative and executive levels, the relationship between the Scottish and United Kingdom tiers of government is a complex one and interdepartmental negotiations commenced in advance of devolution with a view to reaching agreement on joint working arrangements. These negotiations resulted in the publication, in October 1999, of what are collectively referred to as "the concordats", namely:

- A Memorandum of Understanding, which provides for the establishment of a Joint Ministerial Committee bringing together United Kingdom government ministers and representatives of the devolved administrations.
- Four separate overarching concordats providing for "broadly uniform" arrangements for the handling by the various tiers of government of matters with a European Union dimension; matters concerning financial assistance to industry; international relations touching on the responsibilities of the devolved administrations; and statistical work across the United Kingdom.
- A number of bilateral interdepartmental concordats between the United Kingdom government departments and their Scottish counterparts. Similar arrangements exist between United Kingdom government ministers and their opposite numbers in the devolved administrations in Wales and Northern Ireland.

These are not legally binding instruments, and neither the Scottish Ministers nor their colleagues in London are obliged to adhere to their terms. Their purpose is to guide and structure intergovernmental relations, and there are obvious reasons why central and devolved administrations should seek to establish and maintain harmonious working relationships. Ultimately, however, the maintenance of such relationships is a matter of political will rather than legal duty.

---

6. THE COURTS AND THE JUDICIARY

INTRODUCTION

The courts are part of the machinery of state as much as Parliament and the government. Their key function is to determine disputes of fact and law, and in finding and applying the law, the courts are legally subordinate only to the legislative supremacy of the Queen in Parliament as expressed in statutes. This independence of the judicial function is central to the integrity of the judiciary and to the maintenance of the rule of law. The point is captured by section 1 of the Constitutional Reform Act 2005, "this Act does not adversely affect the existing constitutional principle of the rule of law". To that end, section 4 of the Act provides that "the Lord Chancellor, other ministers of the Crown and all with responsibility for matters relating to the judiciary or otherwise to the administration of justice must uphold the continued independence of the judiciary". The same emphasis is seen in Article 6 of the European Convention on Human Rights, which entitles every person, in the determination of his civil rights and obligations or of criminal charges against him, to a fair hearing before an independent and impartial tribunal established by law. The term "tribunal" includes not only the ordinary courts but also disciplinary and other specialised bodies having a judicial function and competence to take legally binding rather than merely advisory decisions. Not only the establishment but also the organisation and functioning of a tribunal must have a basis in law, meaning primary legislation, although aspects of judicial organisation may be delegated to the executive, provided that there are sufficient guarantees against arbitrariness.

Judicial independence is not merely a function of absence of bias on the part of a judge. It also involves freedom from constraint—and the appearance of constraint—by other institutions of the state. It is well-established in the jurisprudence of the European Court of Human Rights that the way in which members of a tribunal are appointed, the term of their office, the presence or absence of guarantees against outside pressure and the mode of their remuneration are all factors relevant to the question whether the tribunal presents a sufficient appearance of independence. In some of these respects, certain aspects of judicial organisation in Scotland have in the past been found wanting.

JUDICIAL OFFICE

Appointments

Judicial appointments in the United Kingdom are a matter for the executive. Lords of Appeal in Ordinary are appointed by the Queen on the advice of the Prime Minister. If the provisions of the Constitutional Reform Bill for the replacement of the House of Lords (in the sense of a court) by a new Supreme Court for the United Kingdom are enacted, Justices of the new court will be appointed by the Queen on the recommendation of the Prime Minister (although the Prime Minister will only be able to recommend the person whose name is notified to him following a statutory process of selection). The Lord President of the Court of Session and the Lord Justice Clerk are also appointed by the Queen on the advice of the Prime Minister, although section 95(2) of the Scotland Act provides that the Prime Minister shall not recommend to the Queen the appointment of any person who has not been nominated by the First Minister; and before making any nomination(s) the First Minister must consult the Lord President and Lord Justice Clerk (unless, in either case, the office is vacant). Under section 95(4), it is for the Queen to appoint persons as Judges of the Court of Session, sheriffs principal or sheriffs on the recommendation of the First Minister. Again, the First

Minister is obliged first to consult the Lord President. In addition, the First Minister consults a Judicial Appointments Board established in 2002 and charged with advertising judicial posts, interviewing candidates and drawing up shortlists for appointment. Section 95(5) provides that any nomination or recommendation the First Minister may make shall also "comply with any requirement ... imposed by virtue of any enactment". Thus the Scottish Parliament may lay down further statutory conditions in relation to such nominations or recommendations. Finally, under section 9 of the District Court (Scotland) Act 1975, as amended by the Scotland Act and by the Bail, Judicial Appointments etc (Scotland) Act 2000, it is for the Scottish Ministers themselves to appoint justices of the peace, in accordance with such regulations as may be made by them and approved by resolution of the Scottish Parliament.

There are, however, certain statutory conditions of eligibility for appointment to judicial office. To be appointed a sheriff principal or sheriff, one must have been legally qualified as a solicitor or advocate for at least 10 years (Sheriff Courts (Scotland) Act 1971, section 5). By virtue of section 7 of the Bail, Judicial Appointments etc (Scotland) Act 2000, which inserts a new section 11A into the 1971 Act, the same conditions of eligibility apply to the appointment of a person as a part-time sheriff. This office is new, and was created in the light of the abolition by the 2000 Act of the office of temporary sheriff following the decision of the High Court of Justiciary in *Starrs v Ruxton* (2000) (see further below). Under Article 19 of the Treaty of Union 1707, appointments to the Court of Session bench are governed by a requirement of at least five years' standing as a member of the Faculty of Advocates. This rule was widened by section 35(1) of the Law Reform (Miscellaneous Provisions) (Scotland) Act 1990, which extends eligibility to sheriffs principal or sheriffs who have held office as such for a continuous period of at least five years, and also to solicitors who have enjoyed rights of audience in both the Court of Session and the High Court of Justiciary for at least five years.

Tenure and pay
The historic tenure on which judges in Scotland hold office is *ad vitam aut culpam*—for life or until blame. This was confirmed by Article 13 of the Claim of Right 1688. Security of tenure was and is regarded as a necessary support for judicial independence, and the principle of lifetime tenure was so firmly entrenched that it was held by the Court of Session to attach to any judicial office as a matter of common law right (*Mackay and Esslemont v Lord Advocate* (1937)).

It is of course open to Parliament to override the presumption of the common law. For example, legislation now prescribes a retirement age of 70 for judges of the Court of Session, sheriffs principal and sheriffs (subject to possible extension to the age of 75 by way of appointment as a "retired judge"). Statutes creating new judicial offices are also apt to define tenure in a manner more limited than *ad vitam aut culpam*. But care must be taken to ensure that limitations on judicial tenure are not such as to give rise to suspicion that the tribunal is not independent. Thus in *Starrs v Ruxton* (2000), the High Court held that, although the initial appointment of temporary sheriffs by the executive was not inherently objectionable, the brevity of their term of office (one year), coupled with the power (albeit unused) under section 11 of the Sheriff Courts (Scotland) Act 1971 to recall a temporary sheriff's commission and the practice of appointing permanent sheriffs from the pool of temporary sheriffs, was fatal to the compatibility of the system with Article 6 of the European Convention on Human Rights. This is not to say that fixed-term appointments are in any way at odds with Article 6. Rather, as Lord Sutherland put it in *Clancy v Caird* (2000):

> "There can be no objection *per se* to the appointment of judges for a fixed term, provided that during that period there is security of tenure which guarantees against interference by the executive in a discretionary or arbitrary manner."

Given that, unlike temporary sheriffs, temporary judges of the Court of Session do enjoy security of tenure during the period of their commission, the Court in *Clancy* dismissed the Article 6 challenge to the independence and impartiality of the temporary judge in that case.

Judicial salaries are an equally important support for judicial independence. For the same reason that tenure is protected, the Act of Settlement 1700 provided that judicial salaries should be "ascertained and established"—fixed by statute and not left open to executive discretion. The determination of the remuneration of judges of the Court of Session, sheriffs principal, sheriffs, members of the Lands Tribunal for Scotland and the Chairman of the Scottish Land Court is reserved to Westminster by section L1 of Schedule 5 to the Scotland Act; but payment of the salaries so determined is charged on the Scottish Consolidated Fund pursuant to section 119 of the Act. The effect of this is that parliamentary authority for payment of judicial salaries is deemed to be permanent and does not need to be reviewed and renewed year by year. Note, however, that section 11A of the Sheriff Courts (Scotland) Act, as inserted by section 7 of the Bail, Judicial Appointments etc (Scotland) Act 2000, provides for part-time sheriffs to be paid by the Scottish Ministers, at a rate determined by them, out of moneys earmarked for the Justice Department of the Scottish Executive.

Dismissal

Until the enactment of the Scotland Act, no procedure was in terms prescribed for the dismissal of a Court of Session judge. Now, however, section 95(6) of the Scotland Act provides that a judge of the Court of Session may be removed from office by the Queen on the recommendation of the First Minister. The First Minister shall only make such a recommendation if the Parliament, on a motion made by the First

Minister, resolves that it should be made. The First Minister may only move the Parliament so to resolve if he has received a reasoned report from a tribunal constituted under section 95(8) concluding that the judge in question is unfit for office by reason of inability, neglect of duty or misbehaviour. Where the judge in question is the Lord President or Lord Justice Clerk, the First Minister must also consult the Prime Minister. He is further obliged to comply with any additional requirements that may be imposed on him by Scottish legislation. Section 95(8) requires provision to be made by or under an Act of the Scottish Parliament for a tribunal of at least three persons, constituted by the First Minister, to investigate and report on a judge's fitness for office and for its reports to be laid before the Parliament. That provision must include provision for the constitution of the tribunal in such circumstances as the First Minister thinks fit or at the request of the Lord President, and for the appointment as chairman of a member of the Judicial Committee of the Privy Council. It may include provision enabling the suspension from office of the judge who is under investigation.

This procedure, which is clearly intended to insulate the process of removing a judge from office from political considerations, borrows a number of the features of the procedure prescribed by section 12 of the Sheriff Courts (Scotland) Act 1971 for the dismissal of sheriffs principal or sheriffs. As amended by the Scotland Act, this provides that the Scottish Ministers may make an order removing a sheriff principal or sheriff from office if, after an inquiry by the Lord President and Lord Justice-Clerk, he or she is found to be unfit for office by reason of inability, neglect of duty or misbehaviour. The order of the Scottish Ministers is laid before the Scottish Parliament and is subject to annulment pursuant to a resolution of the Parliament. Prior to devolution, when the relevant order fell to be made by the Secretary of State for Scotland and laid before the Houses of Parliament, this procedure had been used twice, in 1977 and again in 1992. The procedure for dismissing part-time sheriffs is prescribed by section 11C of the 1971 Act, as inserted by section 7 of the Bail, Judicial Appointments etc (Scotland) Act 2000. Responsibility for deciding whether a part-time sheriff should be removed from office (again, by reason of inability, neglect of duty or misbehaviour) is placed with a tribunal of three persons appointed by the Lord President. The tribunal must be chaired by a Court of Session judge or sheriff principal, and one of its members must be a solicitor or advocate of at least 10 years' standing. The Scottish Ministers may provide in regulations for the suspension of a part-time sheriff who is under investigation.

JUDICIAL INDEPENDENCE

We have seen that the rules relating to judicial appointments, tenure and dismissal may impinge upon judicial independence. That independence might well be threatened by politically motivated appointments, by removal of security of tenure and manipulation of judicial pay, and by powers of dismissal too frequently exercised. This point denotes the fundamental meaning of judicial independence: freedom from constraint by other institutions of the state. Yet judicial independence has a narrower meaning: a judge's independence of mind in relation to the facts of and parties to a case before him. It may also be argued, bearing in mind the exactions of Article 6 of the ECHR, that the concept has a wider meaning of political neutrality and remoteness from controversy.

Absence of bias

In the narrowest sense, judicial independence must mean that a judge is impartial. The common law enshrines a rule against bias (*nemo iudex in causa sua*), because, as Lord Hewart CJ put it in *R v Sussex Justices, ex parte McCarthy* (1924): "It is not merely of some importance, but of fundamental importance that justice should not only be done but should manifestly and undoubtedly be seen to be done."

A judge is automatically disqualified from hearing a case if he has a financial or other economic interest in its outcome (*Dimes v Proprietor of the Grand Junction Canal* (1852)) or if he would be acting as the "judge of his own cause" in the sense that he is in some material way concerned or connected with the subject matter of the case before him (*R v Bow Street Metropolitan Stipendiary Magistrate, ex parte Pinochet Ugarte (No. 2)* (2000)). Beyond the categories of automatic disqualification, a judge may be obliged to decline jurisdiction where the circumstances are such as to give rise to a reasonable suspicion or reasonable apprehension of bias on his part, regardless of whether he is biased in fact. Family or business connections may give rise to such an inference of bias (*Metropolitan Property Co Ltd v Lannon* (1969)), as may evidence of predisposition for or against a party to a case or to the subject matter of a party's arguments (*Bradford v McLeod* (1986); *R v Inner West London Coroner, ex parte Dallaglio* (1996); *Hoekstra v HM Advocate (No 2)* (2000)).

Direct political activities

Court of Session judges, sheriffs principal and sheriffs are disqualified from membership of the House of Commons and of the Scottish Parliament (although a previous political career, whether as an MP, MSP or Law Officer, is no bar to appointment to judicial office). Obvious conflicts of constitutional roles would arise if judges were able to be members of Parliament. Further, by convention, judges should not become involved in party politics. Thus in 1968, a Court of Session judge, Lord Avonside, was forced to resign from a committee set up by the Leader of the Opposition to formulate Conservative policy on the constitutional position of Scotland. In 1977, a sheriff was dismissed after he was found to have used his judicial office as a platform for the promotion of his political beliefs.

The position differs in the House of Lords. Senior judges such as Lords of Appeal in Ordinary, whose jobs carry with them a life peerage, may sit in the House of Lords and contribute to debates on its legislative business. They sit on the cross-benches rather than as adherents of any political party, and while on one view they should maintain an "elective silence" in areas of political controversy, many judges do not see themselves as bound to remain above the political fray. In recent years especially there have been several instances of retired and serving judges openly criticising government policy in debates on legislation. One noteworthy instance of this came in the House of Lords debates on the Scotland Bill, where Lord McCluskey, backed up by Lord Hope and Lord Clyde, vigorously attacked the original provisions relating to the dismissal of Court of Session judges as insufficiently protective of judicial tenure. Lord McCluskey successfully moved an amendment to the clause, leading the government to substitute re-drafted provisions along the lines described above.

It has been said that the House of Lords in its legislative capacity benefits from the participation of the judicial peers. The judicial peers, in return, have said that they themselves benefit from the "wider perspective derived from their closer contact with the legislative process and also from their awareness of debates in the House of matters of current concern." Yet this arrangement sits uneasily not only with notions of judicial independence but also of the doctrine of the separation of powers. Resolving this tension has been one of the main drivers behind the provisions in the Constitutional Reform Act 2005 for the establishment of a new Supreme Court separate from the House of Lords.

Indirect political activities
A number of judicial activities may have indirect political impact. A prominent example is the appointment of judges to conduct public inquiries, such as the Bloody Sunday Inquiry under Lord Saville and the inquiry under Lord Hutton into the death of Dr David Kelly in 2003. The subject matter of such inquiries is invariably controversial. Appointing a judge to conduct them does not remove the political "sting": where a problem is inherently political, there are no neutral solutions. Thus whatever a judge finds or recommends is liable to be viewed as politically partial. Since extra-judicial work on behalf of the government risks undermining the appearance of political impartiality, judges in the United States and Australia generally refuse to serve on government-sponsored inquiries. This emphasises the earlier point that the key to judicial independence is independence from the executive. So far as judicial work of this sort may give the impression of executive influence over the judiciary, it may be inappropriate for judges to undertake it.

Otherwise, judges may contribute to political controversy by expressing their views in the media. In the past, the "Kilmuir Rules" (derived from a letter sent in 1957 by the Lord Chancellor, Lord Kilmuir, to the Director-General of the BBC) discouraged appearances by judges in any medium in view of "the importance of keeping the judiciary insulated from the controversies of the day". In time, both the letter and the spirit of the Kilmuir Rules came to look outdated as judges (Lord Kilmuir included) published memoirs, delivered lectures, wrote for the newspapers and by other means made known their views. In 1987, Lord Mackay LC stated that for the future judges would not be required to consult the Lord Chancellor before making public statements. Since then, several judges have asserted claims to a greater degree of autonomous legitimacy than was thought to exist in the past. Recent extra-judicial writings and speeches indicate the emergence, or articulation, of a particular ethic among the ranks of the senior judiciary, which may indeed be reflected in a number of important recent decisions. It seems that far from feeling bound to remain aloof from controversy, judges regard themselves as *entitled* to engage in controversial issues.

There are risks in this, as two recent cases amply illustrate. *Locabail (UK) Ltd v Bayfield Properties Ltd* (2000) was a decision of the English Court of Appeal on four joined cases. One of these was an appeal by the defendant in a personal injuries action against the judgment of Mr Recorder Braithwaite, QC. The decision of the Recorder, a personal injuries practitioner working primarily on behalf of claimants, was struck down and a re-trial ordered on the basis of four articles written by him on issues of personal injury practice which were said to demonstrate a predisposition to claimants. The Court of Appeal expressly held that the articles were not couched in inappropriate language and did not exhibit such a lack of balance and proportion as to indicate a blinkered approach. Even so, it held that "anyone writing in an area in which he sits judicially has to exercise considerable care not to express himself in terms which indicate that he has preconceived views which are so firmly held that it is not possible for him to try a case with an open mind". It was a caution Lord McCluskey might have observed before publishing an article in the February 6, 2000 edition of the *Scotland on Sunday* to mark his recent retirement from the Court of Session bench. Following his retirement, Lord McCluskey had been appointed to sit as a retired judge, and was sitting in that capacity in the High Court of Justiciary when on January 28 it dismissed devolution issue minutes lodged by four persons convicted of offences under the Customs and Excise Management Act 1979. When the hearing before the High Court continued in March, the petitioners submitted that, in view of the tenor of the comments made in his article about the ECHR, Lord McCluskey could not be regarded as impartial in relation to issues of human rights and that both he and the other judges of the court of which he was a member were disqualified from hearing any further part of their appeal. The issue was passed to a differently constituted bench, which upheld the arguments of the petitioners, set aside the High Court's interlocutors of January 28 and ordered that any further proceedings in the appeal be heard by a new bench: *Hoekstra v HM Advocate (No 2)* (2000).

Judicial independence in perspective

Perhaps the main reason why judicial independence is a matter of such importance is that the discharge of judicial functions impinges not only upon disputes between citizens but also upon disputes between citizen and state. To a great extent, it is judges to whom individuals must look for protection of their rights and liberties against intrusion by the state. If they are to fulfil this role, in particular, their independence of mind and freedom from constraint must be assured.

We have seen that a number of positive steps are taken to achieve this end. Tenure and pay are protected and procedures for dismissal of judges are complex (although some would argue that the appointments process does little to assuage fears of executive interference). Bias is impermissible. But partiality in a wider sense is a different matter. It is unrealistic to expect judges to exist in a vacuum of political neutrality, and it is clear that they do not. Professor Griffith draws on cases on, *e.g.* race and sex discrimination, trade union law and police powers to argue that what may be presented as judicial "neutrality" is not in fact neutral at all. On the contrary, Griffith contends that judges—overwhelmingly white, male, middle-aged, middle-class and privately educated—have an inbuilt ideological persuasion tending to coincide, largely, with Conservative politics. Yet it appears that the chief characteristics of the judicial ethic which has been voiced more prominently in recent years are a suspicion of executive power and a commitment to the protection of individual liberties.

Generalising about judicial politics is probably a pointless exercise. What is indisputable is that judges are not without "political" standpoints to which they sometimes give expression. Does this absence of neutrality, and willingness to engage with controversial questions rather than stand remote from them, undermine judicial independence? It is suggested that, kept within sensible bounds, it does not. As Cane suggests:

> "Public law in general ... exists in a political environment; and the courts in making and applying public law rules perform a variety of political functions. ... It could be argued that ... the ... independence of the judiciary enables the courts to protect certain interests and principles which are of long-term and abiding importance ... from undue encroachment for short-term political reasons."

In so doing, the courts may come into conflict with the executive, but this by itself is not injurious to judicial independence. Quite the reverse: it would tend to emphasise the healthy state of judicial independence, in itself a prerequisite for the rule of law and the checking and balancing of state power.

7. PARLIAMENTARY SUPREMACY

THE NATURE OF THE DOCTRINE

Parliamentary supremacy may (still) be regarded as the fundamental principle of the British constitution. Historically, the status of Acts of Parliament was questionable. In *Dr Bonham's Case* (1610), Coke C.J. held that "when an Act of Parliament is against common right and reason, or repugnant, or impossible to be performed, the common law will control it, and adjudge such act to be void". However, parliamentary supremacy was implicit in the constitutional settlement following the Glorious Revolution. From then on, Parliament was the pre-eminent law maker in the state. Its enactments took precedence over and could change the common law and the prerogative.

In 1885, Dicey referred to parliamentary supremacy as "the very keystone of the law of the constitution" and described it in these terms:

> "Parliament ... has ... the right to make or unmake any law whatever; and ... no person or body is recognised ... as having a right to override or set aside the legislation of Parliament."

The principle therefore has a positive and a negative aspect. On the one hand, Parliament has absolute legislative competence; on the other, no court or other body may question the validity of its legislation.

It is implicit in this that it is the *current* Parliament which is supreme. It therefore follows that any conflict between an Act of the current Parliament and an Act of one of its predecessors must be resolved in favour of the former: the later statute *impliedly repeals* the earlier. In Dicey's theory, the only limitation on Parliament's absolute legislative authority is its inability to bind its successors:

> "The logical reason why Parliament has failed in its endeavours to enact unchangeable enactments is that a sovereign power cannot, while retaining its sovereign character, restrict its own powers by a parliamentary enactment."

In *Ellen Street Estates v Minister of Health* (1934), Maugham L.J. agreed:

> "The legislature cannot ... bind itself as to the form of subsequent legislation, and it is impossible for Parliament to enact that in a subsequent statute dealing with the same subject-matter there can be no implied repeal. If in a subsequent Act Parliament chooses to make it plain that the earlier statute is being to some extent repealed, effect

must be given to that intention just because it is the will of Parliament."

There is evidence supportive of both the positive and negative aspects of Dicey's theory. It is quite rightly said that "one does not establish that Parliament can do anything merely by pointing to a number of things that it has done, however impressive"; but the fact that, so far, Parliament has not done certain things does not necessarily disprove Dicey's theory either. So at least some support for the assertion of unlimited legislative competence may be drawn from the many statutes whereby Parliament has made important constitutional changes (*e.g.* the Reform Act 1832, the Irish Free State (Constitution) Act 1922), enacted retrospective legislation (*e.g.* the War Damage Act 1965), or legislated extra-territorially (*e.g.* the War Crimes Act 1991).

Authority for the negative aspect is found in cases concerning the "enrolled bill rule". In *Edinburgh and Dalkeith Railway Co v Wauchope* (1842) Lord Campbell stated this rule as follows:

> "All that a Court of Justice can do is look to the Parliamentary Roll; if from that it should appear that a Bill has passed both Houses and received the Royal Assent, no Court of Justice can inquire into the mode in which it was introduced into Parliament, nor into what was done previous to its introduction, or what passed in Parliament during its progress ... through Parliament."

More recently, in *Pickin v British Railways Board* (1974), Mr Pickin asked the court to hold a private Act void on the grounds that the Board had procured its enactment by misleading Parliament and that the standing orders of both Houses had not been properly followed. The House of Lords held that the courts had no power to disregard an Act of Parliament, whether public or private, or to inquire into parliamentary procedures. As Willes J. held in *Lee v Bude and Torrington Junction Railway Co* (1871), "[I]f an Act of Parliament has been obtained improperly, it is for the legislature to correct it by repealing it; but so long as it exists as law, the courts are bound to obey it."

The courts have also rejected substantive (as distinct from procedural) arguments to the effect that Parliament lacked authority to legislate. In *Cheney v Conn* (1968) it was argued that assessments of tax under a Finance Act were made partly for a purpose which was unlawful as being contrary to international law. Ungoed-Thomas J. held:

> "What the statute itself enacts cannot be unlawful, because [it] is the highest form of law that is known to this country ... and it is not for the court to say that a parliamentary enactment ... is illegal."

Two basic points should be stressed:

- The doctrine of parliamentary supremacy is a purely legal construct. It denotes the absence of *legal* limitations on Parliament's legislative competence; it does *not* argue that Parliament is unrestrained by political or practical considerations.

• The essence of the doctrine lies in its account of the relationship between Parliament and the courts, and the effect to be given by the courts to Acts of Parliament. The doctrine is a product of the common law: one might therefore say that its continuing truth "lies in the keeping of the courts."

A number of arguments challenge Dicey's theory. These are, first, that the Acts of Union constitute "fundamental law" which Parliament cannot contradict; secondly, that Parliament *has* restricted its legislative competence, notably in the context of the legislation conferring independence on former colonies; thirdly, that even if Parliament cannot restrict its substantive competence, it could bind itself as to the "manner and form" of subsequent legislation; and fourthly, that the UK's accession to the European Communities in 1973 has modified parliamentary supremacy. To these we must now add the recent decision of the Court of Appeal in *R (Jackson) v H.M. Attorney General* (2005), which concerned a challenge to the validity of the Hunting Act 2004 on grounds which the Court of Appeal accepted as justiciable.

THE ACTS OF UNION AS FUNDAMENTAL LAW

It has been argued that the 1707 Treaty of Union, in creating a Parliament. for Great Britain, also limited the powers of the new institution. Parliament cannot enjoy unfettered legislative competence because it was "born unfree". This argument draws on the special nature of the union legislation as fundamental and constituent, and also upon indications in the language of the legislation that parts of it, at least, were intended to be unalterable.

Dicey conceded that the framers of the union legislation may well have sought to give certain provisions more than the ordinary effect of statutes, but "the history of legislation in respect of these very Acts affords the strongest proof of the futility inherent in every attempt of one sovereign legislature to restrain the action of another equally sovereign legislature."

Here Dicey was referring to the Anglo-Irish as well as the Anglo-Scottish union legislation. The Union with Ireland Act 1800 contained language similar to that of the 1707 Treaty. Quite clearly, it failed to have the desired effect: the union itself was dissolved (partially) by an ordinary statute, the Irish Free State (Constitution) Act 1922. While the Anglo-Scottish union remains intact, it is nonetheless true that nearly all of the provisions of the 1707 Treaty have been repealed or amended.

Some Scottish cases contain dicta sympathetic to the fundamental law argument. In *MacCormick v Lord Advocate* (1953) Lord President Cooper observed:

"The principle of the unlimited sovereignty of Parliament is a distinctively English principle which has no counterpart in Scottish constitutional law ... I have difficulty in seeing why it should have been supposed that the new Parliament of Great Britain must inherit all the peculiar characteristics of the English Parliament but none of the Scottish Parliament, as if all that happened in 1707 was that Scottish representatives were admitted to the Parliament of England. That is not what was done."

But, having apparently accepted that certain provisions of the Treaty were to be regarded as unalterable, his Lordship then seemed to doubt whether an allegation of breach of that fundamental law would be "determinable as a justiciable issue in the courts of either Scotland or England". Similarly, in *Gibson v Lord Advocate* (1975), Lord Keith reserved his opinion as to the effect of hypothetical Acts of Parliament purporting to abolish the Church of Scotland or the Court of Session, but held that arguments about whether changes to Scots private law were "for the evident utility" of the subjects in Scotland in accordance with Article XVIII of the Treaty of Union would not be justiciable. More explicitly, Lord Kirkwood stated in *Murray v Rogers* (1992) that "there is ... no machinery whereby the validity of an Act of Parliament can be brought under review by the courts". Thus, even if there is force in the fundamental law argument in the abstract sense, it is of little use if the courts will not treat such issues as justiciable.

THE "END OF EMPIRE" ARGUMENT

Dicey asserted an absence only of legal limitations on Parliament's legislative competence. Yet the distinction between Parliament being legally unlimited and illimitable on the one hand, but politically constrained on the other may seem rather unreal when set against the dismantling of the British Empire. In this context, does it make sense to speak of one Parliament undoing the work of its predecessors by purporting to re-assume legislative authority over former colonies? If it does not make sense, it would seem to follow that earlier Parliaments have bound their successors.

Section 4 of the Statute of Westminster 1931 provided that no future Act of Parliament would extend or be deemed to extend to a Dominion (including Canada, Australia, New Zealand and South Africa) unless it was expressly declared in the Act that the Dominion had requested and consented to its enactment. In enacting section 4, did Parliament deprive itself of the competence to legislate in future for a Dominion, even without the Dominion's request? In *British Coal Corporation v R* (1935), Lord Sankey L.C. remarked that:

"It is doubtless true that the power of the Imperial Parliament to pass on its own initiative any legislation it thought fit extending to Canada remains in theory unimpaired: indeed the Imperial

Parliament could as a matter of abstract law repeal or disregard section 4 of the Statute. But that is theory and has no relation to realities."

Less equivocally still, Stratford ACJ held in the South African case of *Ndlwana v Hofmeyr* (1937) that "freedom once conferred cannot be revoked". The "end of empire" argument suggests, then, that the conferment of independence on former colonies involved an irrevocable abdication by Parliament of its sovereignty in relation to those countries.

If Parliament were to repeal the Canada Act 1982 and purport to legislate again for Canada, the Canadian courts would, no doubt, completely ignore such legislation. But the Diceyan concept of parliamentary supremacy addresses the relationship between Parliament and *United Kingdom* courts: would the courts of Scotland, England and Northern Ireland treat such legislation as valid? The authorities suggest that they would.

For example, in 1965, the government of Southern Rhodesia unilaterally declared independence. In the Southern Rhodesia Act 1965, Westminster reasserted its right to legislate for the territory, and in *Madzimbamuto v Lardner-Burke* (1969), the Privy Council held that emergency regulations made by the rebel regime were void and that the provisions of UK statutes continued to have full legal force in Rhodesia. Be that as it may, the Rhodesian courts did not accept the decisions of the Privy Council as binding on them following the declaration of independence, and held in *R v Ndhlovu* (1968) that the revolutionary constitution of 1965 was the only lawful constitution of Rhodesia. But that does not alter the fact that whatever Acts Parliament might have enacted for Rhodesia, the British courts would have recognised them as valid and obeyed them.

Again, in *Manuel v Attorney General* (1983), Canadian Indian chiefs contended that the Canada Act 1982, which "patriated" the Canadian constitution, was *ultra vires* and void. Megarry V.-C. held:

> "I have grave doubts about the theory of the transfer of sovereignty as affecting the competence of Parliament. ... As a matter of law the courts ... recognise Parliament as being omnipotent in all save the power to destroy its own omnipotence. Under the authority of Parliament the courts of a territory may be released from their legal duty to obey Parliament, but that does not trench on the acceptance by the English courts of all that Parliament does. *Nor must be validity in law be confused with practical enforceability.*"

Although there is no direct Scottish authority on this point, there is little reason to believe that the Scottish courts would not hold likewise.

THE NEW VIEW: "MANNER AND FORM" RESTRICTIONS

It has been argued that, while the doctrine of parliamentary supremacy may prevent Parliament from binding itself as to the content of future legislation, it does not prevent "manner and form" fetters. On this view, should Parliament wish to entrench a particular statute, it could provide in the Act that none of its provisions shall be repealed or amended without, *e.g.* a two-thirds majority vote in both Houses of Parliament.

The evidence relied on for this "new view" of parliamentary supremacy is derived primarily from Commonwealth cases, notably *Attorney General for New South Wales v Trethowan* (1932) and *Bribery Commissioner v Ranasinghe* (1965), both decisions of the Privy Council, and the South African case of *Harris v Minister of the Interior* (1952).

Harris concerned the Separate Representation of Voters Act 1951, passed pursuant to the new apartheid policy by the Union Parliament of South Africa, acting by simple majority, both Houses sitting separately. Voters thereby deprived of their voting rights argued that the Act was invalid because contrary to section 35, South Africa Act 1909 (an Act of the United Kingdom Parliament). Section 35 required certain legislation of the South African Parliament, including the 1951 Act, to be "passed by both Houses of Parliament sitting together, and at third reading ... agreed to by not less than two-thirds of the total number of members of both Houses". The South African government argued that the Union Parliament had since 1909 acquired full legislative sovereignty and so was free to disregard purported limitations on its sovereignty contained in section 35. Unanimously, the court rejected this argument and held the 1951 Act *ultra vires* and void. Centlivres C.J. stated that:

> "A State can unquestionably be sovereign although it has no legislature which is completely sovereign ... In the case of the Union, legal sovereignty is or may be divided between Parliament as ordinarily constituted and Parliament as constituted under [section 35]. Such a division of legislative powers is no derogation from the sovereignty of the Union and the mere fact that that division was enacted in a British statute which is still in force in the Union cannot affect the question in issue. ...The South Africa Act ... created the Parliament of the Union. It is that Act ... which prescribes the manner in which the constituent elements of Parliament must function for the purpose of passing legislation. ... [I]t follows that ... courts of law have the power to declare the Act of 1951 invalid on the ground that it was not passed in conformity with the provisions of section 35."

This passage illustrates the crux of the manner and form theory. In identifying expressions of the sovereign will as an Act of Parliament, the courts need a rule, or rules, of recognition. Among other things, they need a rule defining what we mean by "Parliament" if they are correctly to identify one of its Acts. In *Harris*, the constituent instrument of the Union

Parliament contained such rules for the guidance of the courts in particular instances. Thus where an "Act of Parliament" is enacted by simple majority, both Houses sitting separately, in an area where the governing instrument defines "Parliament" as both Houses sitting together and acting by two-thirds majority, it is both right and logical for the courts to hold that what purports to be an "Act of Parliament" is *not*, in this instance, an Act of Parliament at all.

At one level this tells us little about the United Kingdom Parliament because, as Lord Pearce put it in *Ranasinghe*, "In the United Kingdom there is no governing instrument which prescribes the law-making powers and the forms which are essential to those powers".

But the new view goes further. If the "United Kingdom Parliament" is bound by no definitions in any constituent instrument, its meaning is nonetheless subject to *common law* rules relied on by the courts in the identification of statutes. As a matter of common law, the courts accept that, whatever the Queen in Parliament enacts, both Houses of Parliament sitting separately and acting by simple majority, is law. We know, however, that Parliament can change the common law. It must therefore follow that Parliament can change this common law rule and, in certain circumstances, substitute a different definition of what Parliament is for the purpose of identifying a valid Act of Parliament.

In truth, however, it may not so follow. As Wade wrote in 1955:

> "[T]he rule that the courts obey Acts of Parliament ... is above and beyond the reach of statute ... because it is itself the source of authority of statute. This puts it into a class by itself among rules of the common law ... . The rule of judicial obedience is in one sense a rule of common law, but in another sense—which applies to no other rule of common law—it is the ultimate *political* fact upon which the whole system of legislation hangs. Legislation owes its authority to the rule: the rule does not owe its authority to legislation. To say that Parliament can change the rule ... is to put the cart before the horse. ... The rule is unique in being unchangeable by Parliament- it is changed by revolution, not by legislation; it lies in the keeping of the courts and no Act of Parliament can take it from them."

Such a revolution occurred in Rhodesia, when the Rhodesian courts ceased to recognise British statutes as supreme and relocated their rules of recognition—their criteria of legal validity—in the revolutionary constitution of 1965. The same sort of process occurred in the Glorious Revolution of 1688, where King James was deposed, William and Mary were offered the Crown and the English and Scottish Parliaments asserted their pre-eminence in, respectively, the Bill of Rights and the Claim of Right. By the standards of the time, all of these acts were illegal. Yet in 1688 the pre-existing legal order was comprehensively overturned. By what standard then can it be said that what happened in 1688, and what has happened since, is legal? The answer to this lies in the acquiescence of the courts in the "break in legal continuity" occasioned by new political realities and in their acceptance of a new criterion of legal validity, namely the legal supremacy of Parliament.

Does this mean that, however much Parliament may wish to entrench a measure in the future, it is simply unable to do so—or unable to do so without a "revolution"? Professor Wade himself refuted this notion:

> "Even without a [break in legal continuity] there might be a shift in judicial loyalty if we take into account the dimension of time … [N]ew generations of judges might come to accept that there had been a new constitutional settlement based on common consent and long usage, and that the old doctrine of sovereignty was ancient history … The judges would then be adjusting their doctrine to the facts of constitutional life, as they have done throughout history."

The courts have already made such an adjustment in respect of the impact of Community law, as we shall presently see. However, one cannot pass from the "manner and form" theory without reference to the Court of Appeal decision in *R (Jackson) v HM Attorney General* (2005). There, supporters of hunting sought to challenge the validity of the Hunting Act 2004. The 2004 Act was enacted under the procedure prescribed by the Parliament Act 1911, as amended by the Parliament Act 1949. It will be remembered that the latter Act reduced the Lords' delaying power from two years to one. It was itself enacted under and in accordance with the 1911 Act. The essence of the argument for the applicants was that legislation passed under the 1911 Act is not primary but subordinate legislation; that powers given by an enabling statute (here the 1911 Act) cannot be enlarged or modified by the body so enabled (namely, Parliament as constituted by the Commons and Sovereign alone) save by express words of authorisation; and that on a true construction of the 1911 Act, it did not authorise the Commons and Sovereign to remove or attenuate the conditions on which their law-making power was granted. Having satisfied itself that the matter was even justiciable, the Court of Appeal held that the challenge must fail on the basis that the 1911 Act did permit of its own amendment to the extent contained in the 1949 Act. Although much opposition had been voiced to the principle of the 1949 Act during its parliamentary passage, it was accepted both in the Commons and the Lords that the government could use the procedure contained in the 1911 Act to pass the bill despite the opposition of the Lords. Further, four statutes, including the Hunting Act itself, had been enacted under the amended Parliament Act procedure since 1949. These the Court of Appeal took to be "cogent examples of the general recognition by Parliament, the Queen, the courts and the populace, that the 1949 Act was a proper exercise of sovereign legislative power and that the same is true of legislation enacted pursuant to the provisions of the 1949 Act". As Professor Wade put it:

"[T]he seat of sovereign power is not to be discovered by looking at Acts of Parliament but by looking at the courts and discovering to whom they give their obedience. ... [Sovereignty] is a political fact for which no purely legal authority can be constituted even though an Act of Parliament is passed for that very purpose."

For the Court of Appeal, the restrictions on the exercise of the powers of the House of Lords that the 1949 Act purported to make had been so widely recognised and relied upon that they had acquired the status of "political fact". It is significant, however, that the Court of Appeal in *Jackson* was not prepared to go further than hold that the amendment made by in the 1949 Act was, in effect, within the powers of the Commons and Sovereign under the 1911 Act. In particular, the Court of Appeal accepted the applicants' argument that legislation enacted pursuant to the 1911 Act (before its amendment and since) had the character of delegated or subordinate legislation. The 1911 Act effected a radical constitutional resettlement in removing the power of the House of Lords, in given circumstances, to block legislation approved by the Commons. Various exceptions were made to this general rule, many of which were protective or precautionary in nature. In particular, section 2(1) of the Act provided that the Parliament Act procedure was not to be used to enact legislation extending the life of Parliament beyond five years. Any such legislation, in other words, would require the consent of Parliament as *fully* constituted. In the opinion of the Court of Appeal, any attempt to circumvent the will of Parliament as expressed in section 2(1)—by using the Parliament Act procedure to delete the words "Bill containing any provision to extend the maximum duration of Parliament beyond five years" and then passing further legislation under that procedure to extend the life of Parliament—would be invalid. As Lord Pearce had held in *Ranasinghe*, a constitutional settlement may be altered or amended by the legislature if the regulating instrument so provides and if the terms of its provisions are complied with. Whether or not this is so depends on the proper construction of the regulating instrument, here the 1911 Act. While the Court of Appeal were able to find that the limited alteration to the time limits effected under the 1911 Act in 1949 was within the scope of the 1911 Act properly construed, there are limitations on the competence of Parliament as redefined for the purposes of the 1911 Act which the courts have jurisdiction to enforce (even, implicitly, to the extent of striking down legislation enacted outwith that sphere of competence).

THE EFFECT OF EUROPEAN COMMUNITY LAW

The United Kingdom became a member of the European Communities on January 1, 1973. Community law is derived primarily from the founding treaties which established the European Communities, including the EC Treaty signed at Rome in 1957; and from the treaties which have since amended the founding treaties, notably the Single European Act 1986; the Treaty on European Union signed at Maastricht in 1992; the 1997 Treaty of Amsterdam, which takes the process of European integration still further; and the 2001 Treaty of Nice. Community law also consists of acts of the Community institutions which have legal force: regulations, directives and decisions. Treaties entered into by the Community with third states also become part of Community law; and the European Court of Justice (ECJ) has held that rules of Community law may also be derived from "general principles of law common to the member states".

On accession to Treaties, member states are obliged by Article 10 of the EC Treaty to "take all appropriate measures ... to ensure fulfilment of the obligations arising out of this Treaty or resulting from action taken by the institutions of the Community". As a matter of British constitutional law, treaties signed and ratified by the government have no domestic legal force unless and until incorporated by Act of Parliament. The European Communities Act 1972 was therefore enacted to incorporate Community law and to enable the United Kingdom to fulfil the further obligations of membership. Section 1 defines the Community treaties being incorporated and provides that the government may by Order in Council declare other treaties to be Community treaties for the purposes of the Act. Section 2 then provides for the whole body of Community law, including future accretions to that body of law, to be applied in United Kingdom courts. Section 2(4) is especially worthy of note. It provides that "any enactment passed or to be passed ... shall be construed and have effect subject to the foregoing provisions of this section", that is, subject to Community law as incorporated in accordance with section 2(1). Section 3 provides that in all legal proceedings in the UK, any questions as to the meaning or effect of Community law shall be determined in accordance with the jurisprudence of the ECJ. These provisions will be amended by the enactment and entry into force of the European Union Bill, before Parliament at the time of writing, in order to enable the Treaty establishing a Constitution for Europe to have legal effect in the UK (the bill also makes provision for a referendum to be held on the European Constitution; this is expected to take place in 2006).

What then is the relationship between Community law and national law? It must be stressed at the outset that Community law is, to put it mildly, a distinctive species of international law. As the ECJ asserted in *Van Gend en Loos* (1963), "[t]he Community constitutes a new legal order of international law *for the benefit of which states have limited their sovereign rights*".

This pronouncement of the autonomy of Community law was shortly followed by a pronouncement of its primacy in *Costa v ENEL* (1964):

"The transfer by the states from their domestic legal systems to the Community legal system of the rights and obligations arising under the Treaty carries with it a *permanent limitation of their sovereign rights, against which a subsequent unilateral act incompatible with the concept of the Community cannot prevail.*"

The ECJ later held in *Internationale Handelsgesellschaft* (1970) that Community law in all its forms prevails even over conflicting provisions of national constitutions. It also prevails whether the conflicting national law was made before or after the relevant provisions of Community law, as the ECJ made clear in *Simmenthal* (1978):

> "[E]very national court must ... apply Community law in its entirety and protect rights which the latter confers on individuals, and must accordingly set aside any provision of national law which may conflict with it, whether prior or subsequent to the Community rule."

Thus where Community law and national law clash, it is the duty of national courts to "disapply" national law to the extent of the conflict. The challenge to traditional notions of parliamentary supremacy—that Parliament has unlimited legislative competence, and that no court is able to question an Act of Parliament—is obvious. The question is whether there is any way of reconciling Diceyan doctrine with the primacy of Community law.

Without the European Communities Act 1972, Community law would never have become part of the law of the United Kingdom. It was that Act which, by incorporating Community law, made it domestically binding and enforceable. However, the very fact that an Act of Parliament was necessary to achieve this would seem to leave Community law vulnerable to a future Act of Parliament which contradicted it. The role of national courts as traditionally understood is to give effect to the latest expression of the sovereign will of Parliament. That, one might argue, remains the case even though the 1972 Act itself directs the United Kingdom courts to enforce any measures of Community law which have created enforceable individual rights.

For practical purposes, the courts have effected a reconciliation by adopting a special principle of statutory construction in this field. In *Macarthys v Smith* (1979), a conflict existed between Article 119 of the Treaty of Rome, concerning equal pay, and section 1, Equal Pay Act 1970. Lord Denning MR held that:

> "Under section 2(1) and (4) of the European Communities Act 1972 the principles laid down in the Treaty are 'without further enactment' to be given legal effect in the United Kingdom; and have priority over 'any enactment passed or to be passed' by our Parliament ... In construing our statute, we are entitled to look to the Treaty as an aid to its construction; but not only as an aid but as an overriding force. If ... it should appear that our legislation is deficient or is inconsistent with Community law by some oversight of our draftsmen then it is our bounden duty to give priority to Community

law. Such is the result of section 2(1) and (4) of the European Communities Act 1972."

Thus the courts will presume that any inconsistency with Community law contained in a British statute was unintended and accidental. The courts are therefore doing no more than fulfilling Parliament's real and genuine intention—to comply with Community law—in overriding the domestic provision.

In *Macarthys*, however, the incompatibility was contained in a statute pre-dating the European Communities Act 1972. It could therefore be argued that section 1 of the Equal Pay Act 1970 had been impliedly repealed by the 1972 Act and, as such, by Community law. More important is the question of how the courts treat a subsequent statute which conflicts with Community law. This was the issue in the famous *Factortame* case. A number of English companies whose management and shareholders were primarily Spanish nationals lost their right to exploit the United Kingdom's fishing quota when the Merchant Shipping Act 1988 made the right conditional on nationality requirements they were unable to meet. The companies argued that the Act was unlawful as being in breach of the Treaty of Rome. The ECJ held in *R v Transport Secretary, ex parte Factortame (No. 2)* (1991) that the legislation was incompatible with Community law. The case was returned to the House of Lords, where Lord Bridge held:

"Some public comments on the decision of the Court of Justice … have suggested that this was a novel and dangerous invasion by a Community institution of the sovereignty of the United Kingdom Parliament. But such comments are based on a misconception. If the supremacy within the European Community of Community law over the national law of member states was not always inherent in the EEC Treaty it was certainly well-established in the jurisprudence of the Court of Justice long before the United Kingdom joined the Community. *Thus whatever limitation of its sovereignty Parliament accepted when it enacted the European Communities Act 1972 was entirely voluntary.* Under the terms of the 1972 Act it has always been clear that it was the duty of a United Kingdom court, when delivering final judgment, to override any rule of national law found to be in conflict with any directly enforceable rule of Community law."

The House of Lords has since held that there is no constitutional bar which prevents an individual directly seeking judicial review of primary legislation which is alleged to be in breach of Community law before the United Kingdom courts (*R v Employment Secretary, ex parte Equal Opportunities Commission* (1995)).

Where does this leave us? As a matter of national law, the courts have accepted the supremacy of Community law over Acts of Parliament whether enacted prior or subsequent to the relevant Community provisions. In either case, it is presumed that Parliament did not intend to contravene Community law. Thus it is not open to Parliament *impliedly* to repeal Community law or, for that matter, the European Communities Act 1972 (a British statute which, it would seem, is resistant to implied repeal). The principle of parliamentary supremacy has therefore been modified to this extent: we must now say that Parliament has unlimited legislative competence and no court may question or set aside an Act of Parliament *except* where Community law applies, in which case Community law prevails and the courts have jurisdiction to declare an Act of Parliament to be incompatible with Community law.

Factortame left two matters open: first, whether Parliament might *expressly* derogate from Community law; and secondly, whether what was true of the European Communities Act 1972 might also be true of other statutes. Lord Denning MR addressed the first of these questions in *Macarthys*:

> "If the time should come when our Parliament deliberately passes an Act with the intention of repudiating the Treaty or any provision of it or intentionally of acting inconsistently with it and says so in express terms then I should have thought that it would be the duty of our courts to follows the statute of our Parliament."

The contrary view is that Parliament cannot lawfully depart from Community law expressly or otherwise: if the UK wishes to depart from its obligations as a member state, it must negotiate for release from the European Union and for the restoration of the sovereignty it transferred to that institution on accession. Such arguments were advanced for the respondent in *Thoburn v Sunderland City Council* (2003), in suggesting that by dint of Community law the doctrine of implied repeal had no application to the 1972 Act. Laws L.J. agreed that the provisions of the 1972 Act could not be impliedly repealed, but did not consider that to be a consequence of Community law. Rather, it was the result of domestic law itself:

> "The common law has in recent years allowed, or rather created, exceptions to the doctrine of implied repeal, a doctrine which was always the common law's own creature. There are now classes or types of legislative provision which cannot be repealed by mere implication. These instances are given, and can only be given, by our own courts, to which the scope and nature of parliamentary sovereignty are ultimately confided. The courts may say—and have said—that there are certain circumstances in which the legislature may only enact what it desires to enact if it does so by express, or at any rate, specific provision. The courts have in effect so held in the field of European law itself in *Factortame*."

In other words, if Parliament wishes to legislate contrary to Community law, it may do so but must do so in such a way that its intention is plain.

In that event, the duty of the courts according to Laws L.J. would be to submit to the legislative will because "the fundamental legal basis of the United Kingdom's relationship with the EU rests with the domestic, not the European, legal powers".

As to the second issue identified above, whether it is only the European Communities Act 1972 that benefits from this dispensation from implied repeal, Laws L.J. held as follows:

> "In the present state of its maturity the common law has come to recognise that there exist rights which should properly be classified as constitutional or fundamental. And from this a further insight follows. We should recognise a hierarchy of Acts of Parliament: as it were 'ordinary' statutes and 'constitutional' statutes ... 'Ordinary' statutes may be impliedly repealed. 'Constitutional' statutes may not."

Amongst the family of "constitutional" statutes Laws L.J. placed the legislation providing for the Anglo-Scottish Union of 1707, legislation to enlarge the franchise, including the Great Reform Act of 1832, and the Scotland Act and Human Rights Act, both enacted in 1998. The Human Rights Act adds a further dimension to our analysis of the contemporary status of the doctrine of parliamentary supremacy, for it provides that, where provisions of an Act of Parliament are incompatible with one or more of the "Convention rights", certain higher courts may make "declarations of incompatibility" in respect of those provisions. It is important to note, however, that incompatibility with Community law or the Convention rights does not involve the *invalidity* of the domestic statute. In either context, a declaration of incompatibility is exactly that, and does not affect the validity, continuing operation or enforcement of the provision in question (albeit that in normal circumstances government and Parliament would respond to the finding of incompatibility by taking the necessary corrective action). Moreover, while Community law and the Convention rights provide criteria for the review of primary legislation, they have that status by virtue of two Acts of Parliament, the European Communities Act 1972 and the Human Rights Act 1998; and what Parliament has given it may also take away (if only, according to *Thoburn*, by express words or necessary implication).

In conclusion, we may say this. Provided Parliament speaks clearly, it remains free to make or unmake any law whatsoever, and although the courts may pronounce on the compatibility of its enactments with Community law or the Convention rights, they cannot set those enactments aside. Thus there has been a shift in the doctrine of parliamentary supremacy. It does not, however, constitute the "break in legal continuity" that would be required to deprive the doctrine of its status as the "top rule" of our constitutional law.

8. PRINCIPLES OF CONSTITUTIONAL GOVERNMENT

The term "constitutionalism" denotes a particular conception of the relationship between the state and individual citizens. It is both a descriptive concept and a prescriptive one: descriptive in that it is reflected in actual constitutional practice; prescriptive in that it also guides and influences constitutional practice. Constitutionalism has a long historical pedigree, for it has been recognised since ancient times that while genuine individual freedom in a community of persons requires rule-making and rule-enforcing institutions, the powers of government may be used not to promote individual freedom but to restrict and oppress it. Theories of constitutionalism therefore seek to reconcile the need for order and government with the preservation of liberty. This reconciliation is achieved, broadly speaking, by using law to empower, guide and restrain both government and citizens. Crucial principles bound up in the notion of constitutionalism are the rule of law and the separation of powers.

THE RULE OF LAW

The basic idea of the rule of law is the subjection of power to legal limits. In Dicey's view, the rule of law was one of the cornerstones of the constitution and had been since the Revolution of 1688 put an end to the claims of the Stuarts to rule by prerogative right and ushered in the modern era of parliamentary supremacy. Judicial affirmation of the rule of law in this sense came in *Entick v Carrington* (1765). There, the Secretary of State had issued a warrant ordering the King's Messengers to break into Entick's house and seize his books and papers. When sued for damages, it was claimed that the warrant was valid authority for the Messengers' actions, a power of seizure being necessary for the ends of government. Lord Camden C.J. rejected this argument in the following terms:

> "[E]very invasion of private property ... is a trespass. No man can set his foot upon my ground without my licence, but he is liable to an action ... If he admits the fact, *he is bound to show by way of justification that some positive law has empowered or excused him. The justification is submitted to the judges, who are to look into the books, and see if such a justification can be maintained by the text of the statute law, or principles of the common law* ... It is said that it is necessary for the ends of government to lodge such a power with a state officer ... but with respect to the argument of state necessity, or to a distinction that has been aimed at between state offences and

others, the common law does not understand that kind of reasoning, nor do our books take notice of any such distinctions."

In his exposition of the rule of law, Dicey went beyond this basic principle of legality. There are three facets to Dicey's theory:

- He took the rule of law to mean, first, "the absolute supremacy or predominance of regular law as opposed to the influence of arbitrary power". Arbitrariness, prerogative, even "wide discretionary authority on the part of the government" he regarded as incompatible with the rule of law.
- The rule of law also denoted equality before the law, meaning "the equal subjection of all classes to the ordinary law of the land administered by the ordinary law courts". Where the rule of law was observed, officials and private citizens alike were subject to the same legal rules before the same courts.
- Thirdly, the rule of law meant that "with us the law of the constitution ... [is] not the source but the consequence of the rights of individuals, as defined and enforced by the courts." Dicey regarded the British constitution as being the product of the ordinary law, developed by the courts on a case by case basis, as contrasted with a constitutional order superimposed from above in the manner of a written constitution. Individual rights were not conferred by a constitutional document, but were secured by the availability of ordinary legal remedies to those whose rights had been unlawfully infringed.

Many criticisms may be made of Dicey's account. First, few would accept today that discretionary governmental powers are incompatible with the rule of law. In the modern interventionist state—as distinct from the "nightwatchman state" of the 19th century—discretionary powers are both prevalent and necessary. Moreover, as discretionary powers have their source in statutes—"regular law"—they have unquestionable legal pedigree themselves. Constitutionalism does not require us to get rid of discretionary power, but to develop appropriate legal and political controls by which to regulate its exercise.

Secondly, Dicey's emphasis on equality before the law stemmed from his aversion to the separation of public and private law in France. He considered that the French system of administrative courts protected officials and disfavoured the citizen. This viewpoint is misconceived. Separate administrative courts may offer protection to the citizen as well as, if not better than, ordinary courts. In any event, the Crown enjoys a number of immunities in the United Kingdom which diminish the force of Dicey's assertion of equality before the law (see *e.g. Lord Advocate v Dumbarton DC* (1990), which affirmed the rule that the Crown is not subject to any burden imposed by a statute unless the statute says it is to be bound in express terms or by necessary implication).

As to Dicey's third meaning of the rule of law, it is questionable whether his "judge-made constitution" was adequate to the task of protecting individual freedom from state power. Ordinary common law remedies were of no help in *Malone v Metropolitan Police Commissioner* (1979). There, with the permission of the Post Office (which was at that time in charge of telecommunications), the police had tapped Mr Malone's telephone. They had no positive legal authority to do this, but there was nothing to stop them. As tapping telephones involved no invasion of property rights, and since the common law recognised no right of privacy, Mr Malone was denied a remedy (although in *Malone v United Kingdom* (1984) the European Court of Human Rights held that the United Kingdom was in breach of the right of privacy enshrined in Article 8 of the European Convention). Furthermore, as Acts of Parliament override the common law, it has always been possible for Parliament to restrict or remove fundamental freedoms by statute. Parliamentary supremacy was the other cornerstone of the Diceyan constitution, but if the rule of law means merely that oppressive executive actions be clothed with legality by statute, it amounts to little guarantee of individual liberty in a system where Parliament is supreme and where it is possible for the government to harness that supremacy to its own ends. However, the enactment and entry into force of the Human Rights Act 1998 has radically altered this position. As we shall see, that Act obliges all public authorities (including the courts) to act consistently with fundamental rights and requires all legislation to be read and given effect, so far as possible, in a manner compatible with such rights. Moreover, if it is not possible to read a particular piece of legislation in this way, certain higher courts have the power to make a "declaration of incompatibility" in respect of it.

The rule of law has rightly been described as a principle of "institutional morality", and it has great resonance and moral authority as a tool of criticism of constitutional practice. Not surprisingly, then, there has been much debate about the content of the principle and about how much work it can be made to do. A distinction to be drawn here is that between *formal* and *substantive* conceptions of the rule of law. Formal conceptions, as Raz explains, focus on matters of procedure rather than matters of substance or the content of laws:

> "If the rule of law is the rule of the good law, then to explain its nature is to propound a complete social philosophy. But if so, the term lacks any useful function. We have no need to be converted to the rule of law just in order to discover that to believe in it is to believe that good should triumph."

The formal rule of law therefore embodies politically neutral values, which because of their neutrality may be universally acceptable. Laws should be general, not discriminatory; open, not secret; clear, not obscure in their meaning; stable, not forever changing; and prospective rather than retrospective in application. To ensure conformity with these standards, the independence of the judiciary must be assured, the principles of natural justice must be observed and access to justice must be guaranteed. Compliance with these values enables officials and private citizens alike to plan their conduct in a rational way.

Critics of this approach argue that such formalism is compatible with iniquitous legal systems such as those of the Third Reich or South Africa under apartheid. It has also been said that the formal rule of law is a "legitimating device" which blinds people to real, substantive inequalities in society and so shores up the control of a political élite. Substantive conceptions of the rule of law therefore subscribe to the values included in formal conceptions. However, to quote Craig:

> "[T]hey wish to take the doctrine further. Certain substantive rights are said to be based on, or derived from, the rule of law. The concept is used as the foundation for these rights, which are then used to distinguish between 'good' laws, which comply with such rights, and 'bad' laws, which do not."

In defence of the formalists, however, substantive conceptions could be accused of attempting to attach the moral persuasion of the term "rule of law" to their own preferred political theories, thereby rendering the doctrine unhelpfully contingent upon subjective viewpoints. In insisting on the independent and general functions of the rule of law, formalists have made clear that the rule of law is not the only attribute which a "good" constitution should possess. There are other worthy attributes to which to aspire—democracy, justice, equality, a Bill of Rights—but these are not to be confused with, or seen to be required by, the rule of law itself.

THE SEPARATION OF POWERS

The classic statements of the separation of powers doctrine came in the 17th and 18th centuries. In his *Second Treatise on Civil Government* (1690), Locke said:

> "It may be too great a temptation to human frailty, apt to grasp at power, for the same persons who have the power of making laws to have also in their hands the power to execute them."

In *The Spirit of the Laws* (1748), Montesquieu wrote:

> "In every government there are three sorts of power ... that of making laws, that of executing public affairs and that of adjudicating on crimes and individual causes ... When the legislative and executive powers are united in the same person or in the same body of magistrates, there can be no liberty ... Again, there is no liberty if the power of judging is not separated from the legislative and

executive ... There would be an end to everything if the same man or the same body ... were to exercise those three powers."

Implicit in this is the crucial evil that the separation of powers doctrine seeks to avoid: the monopolisation of the powers of the state in too few hands, with all that that implies in terms of loss of liberty. The powers of the state are therefore divided into three categories—legislative, executive and judicial powers—and, according to the doctrine, separate institutions should exercise these powers.

Montesquieu was greatly influenced in his account of the separation of powers by his observation of the post-1688 British constitution. 20th century critics have argued that British constitutional practice does not in fact reflect any thoroughgoing separation of powers, and indeed never did. It is true that Montesquieu failed to remark the emergence of the Cabinet system—our parliamentary executive—and the difficulties this would create for a "pure" rendering of the separation of powers. But Montesquieu did not, in fairness, insist on an absolute division of the functions of the state between separate institutions. This is evident from his acceptance of the need for "checks and balances". This term refers to means by which the institutions of the state could influence and restrict each other's actions, and would seem to imply some scope for one institution trespassing in the sphere of one or both of the others. In short, 20th century criticism of the doctrine has failed to do justice to the contribution which it has made to the maintenance of liberty and the continuing need by constitutional means to restrain abuse of governmental power.

In descriptive terms, nevertheless, there is at first glance much to support the view that the separation of powers is not a feature of the British constitution. There are obvious institutional overlaps. The Sovereign, in a formal sense, is part of the legislature, executive and judiciary, as is the Lord Chancellor—for the time being—in a rather more practical sense. The government is drawn from Parliament. But while there may be some crossover in terms of personnel, are functional divisions nevertheless observed?

The primary legislative function is vested in the Queen in Parliament. Yet certain autonomous powers of the Crown to legislate by Order in Council survived the 1688 settlement. Legislative powers are frequently delegated by Parliament to executive bodies such as ministers and local authorities, even to the extent of authorising ministers to amend or repeal primary legislation. In matters of Community law, the Council of Ministers and European Commission legislate for the United Kingdom. And in a more basic sense, it may be said that the primary legislative function is only formally vested in the Queen in Parliament. Government bills dominate that part of parliamentary time devoted to the legislative process and no other bills will be passed without government support. If the government has a working Commons majority, it is very exceptional for its legislation to be rejected by the Commons. The powers of the

House of Lords to amend legislation passed by the Commons are limited, and its consent may be dispensed with anyway under the Parliament Acts. By convention, the Queen never refuses the Royal Assent. In an *effective* sense, then, it might be more accurate to say that the primary legislative function is at the disposal of the government of the day.

The executive function is residual, comprising anything which is not clearly legislative or judicial. Yet the executive does possess legislative and judicial powers as well. The relationship of executive and legislature we have noted. The relationship of executive and judiciary is a little more subtle. By and large, the executive does not seek to exercise essential judicial functions, such as the conduct of trials, although it has run into trouble before the European Court of Human Rights for assuming powers which, under the European Convention, should be subject to judicial decision. In the past, moreover, as the state assumed increasing powers in the areas of economic regulation and social welfare, it was often decided to entrust disputes arising out of new statutory schemes not to the ordinary courts but to ministers directly, or to administrative tribunals. The functions of these executive bodies were, at least, "quasi-judicial". In time, this process gave rise to concern and the government appointed a Committee on Administrative Tribunals and Inquiries under the chairmanship of Sir Oliver Franks. The Franks Report in 1957, which led to legislation, established a number of important principles applicable to "administrative justice" of this sort, among them the independence of administrative tribunals from the government department concerned with their work, and the application of truly judicial standards of openness, fairness and impartiality to their procedures. There may be sensible reasons for entrusting particular disputes to tribunals, but the Franks Report made clear that where this is done, such bodies are to be regarded as part of the machinery of justice and must act accordingly. Nowadays, this is a message powerfully reinforced by the requirements of the right to a hearing before an independent and impartial tribunal under Article 6 of the European Convention on Human Rights.

Do the courts exercise legislative functions; and does Parliament exercise judicial functions? The involvement of the Lord Chancellor and Lords of Appeal in Ordinary in the legislative business of the House of Lords is far less significant than the role of the judiciary in interpreting legislation and in applying and developing the common law. Judges do not like the term "judicial legislation", but sometimes it is not inapposite. By contrast, Parliament exercises only a limited judicial function in relation to the enforcement of its privileges and punishment of breaches of privilege.

However, it is misleading to concentrate exclusively on how far our constitutional arrangements mirror a pure theory of the separation of powers when assessing the validity of the doctrine in the United Kingdom. The separation of powers is not only a descriptive doctrine. It is prescriptive too: it says what *should* happen if the monopolisation of state power is to be avoided. That is the motivating force behind the doctrine, and it is perhaps more instructive to look for instances of inter-institutional tension—checks and balances—which may be positively enhanced by departures from an over-rigid separation of powers. So, for example, the fact that the government is drawn from Parliament and is responsible to it enables the legislature to scrutinise, criticise and sometimes even oust the government (although how far and how well Parliament actually does any of these things is questionable). The Franks Report, mentioned above, may be seen as a powerful vindication of the continuing relevance of the reasoning underpinning the separation of powers doctrine. Perhaps the most important and systematic check and balance in modern times is judicial review of administrative action. Since the 1960s, enormous advances have been made in this field, now reinforced by the operation of the Human Rights Act 1998. Judicial review was a vital, if belated, response to the great expansion in the power of the executive in the first half of the 20th century; today, the supervisory jurisdiction of the courts is deployed with impressive intensity to ensure that the powers of the executive are exercised within their legal limits and in accordance with judge-made principles of good administration. The courts do not have the power to review the validity of primary legislation, but even here the winds of change have been felt: an Act of Parliament incompatible with Community law may be disapplied by the courts, and the courts now have jurisdiction under the Human Rights Act to declare an Act of Parliament incompatible with the rights therein enshrined.

It is fitting to conclude this chapter with reference to judicial review, for it is clear that the courts could not perform this vital aspect of the judicial function if subjected to undue interference by either the executive or the legislature. The British version of the separation of powers may be messy and imperfect, but it does recognise the fundamental importance of judicial independence, which is necessary not only in separation of powers terms but also for the maintenance of the rule of law and constitutional government in general.

---

9. HUMAN RIGHTS

INTRODUCTION

The object of the Human Rights Act 1998, as set out in its Preamble, is "to give further effect to the rights and freedoms guaranteed under the European Convention on Human Rights". The European Convention was adopted by the Council of Europe in 1950 and entered into force in 1953.

A product of the post-war period of reconciliation and reconstruction in Europe, the Convention was substantially drafted by British lawyers and reflected the body of civil and political freedoms supposedly embedded in the legal systems of the United Kingdom. Yet the British government of the day came close to not ratifying the Convention at all. It was not until 1966 that the government accorded to the citizens of the United Kingdom the right of individual petition (the right, renewed every five years, to take a case against the state to the European Court of Human Rights in Strasbourg) and, despite mounting demands for "incorporation" of the Convention and increasing disenchantment with the capacity of the domestic courts to protect civil liberties and fundamental rights, it was not until 1997 that a political party committed to incorporation actually took office. The Human Rights Act 1998 was duly enacted to "bring the Convention rights home" and enable litigants to claim and enforce their rights directly before the national courts.

The principal provisions of the Human Rights Act entered partially into force in Scotland in 1999 by virtue of the Scotland Act, which makes compliance with the Convention rights a condition of the legality of Acts of the Scottish Parliament and of actions and decisions of members of the Scottish Executive. The Act came fully into force, throughout the UK, on 2 October 2000.

THE EUROPEAN CONVENTION ON HUMAN RIGHTS

The UK is obliged by Article 1 of the Convention to "secure" the rights laid down therein. These include:

- The right to life (Article 2).
- Freedom from torture and inhuman or degrading treatment or punishment (Article 3).
- Freedom from slavery, servitude and forced labour (Article 4).
- The right to liberty and security of one's person (Article 5).
- The right to a fair trial (Article 6).
- Freedom from retroactive criminal convictions or penalties (Article 7).
- The right to respect for one's private and family life, home and correspondence (Article 8).
- Freedom of thought, conscience and religion (Article 9).
- Freedom of expression (Article 10).
- Freedom of assembly and association (Article 11).
- The right to marry and found a family (Article 12).

Under Article 13, an effective remedy before a national authority must be secured to those whose rights and freedoms as set forth in the Convention have been violated. Under Article 14, the enjoyment of the rights and freedoms enshrined in the Convention must be secured to all without discrimination on any grounds such as sex, race, colour, language, religion, political or other opinion, national or social origin, association with a national minority, property, birth or other status. Since 1950, the Convention has been supplemented several times by the addition of Protocols, such as the First Protocol signed at Paris in 1952. This enshrines the right to the peaceful enjoyment of one's possessions, the right to education and the right to take part in regular free elections held by secret ballot.

Few of the Convention rights are absolute. Even the right to life may be infringed: "a) in defence of any person from unlawful violence; b) in order to effect a lawful arrest or to prevent the escape of a person unlawfully detained; c) in action lawfully taken for the purpose of quelling a riot or insurrection". Articles 8 to 11 may be subject to limitations which are prescribed by law and which are necessary in a democratic society in the interests of, for example, national security, the protection of public order or the prevention of disorder and crime, the protection of public health, safety or morals, the protection of the rights and freedoms of others and the prevention of disclosure of confidential information. Moreover, a state may derogate under Article 15 from its obligations under the Convention in time of war or other public emergency threatening the life of the nation, to the extent strictly required by the exigencies of the situation. Only Article 2 (except in respect of deaths resulting from lawful acts of war), Article 3, Article 4(1) and Article 7 are non-derogable.

THE PROCEDURE OF THE EUROPEAN COURT OF HUMAN RIGHTS

In the past, the only way of vindicating one's rights under the European Convention was to make a complaint to the European Court of Human Rights, and individuals may still wish to invoke their right of petition following the entry into force of the Human Rights Act if they consider that the national courts have failed fully to protect their rights. The procedures of the European Court were comprehensively changed by the entry into force of Protocol 11 to the Convention in November 1998. Protocol 11 established a permanent court which assumed the jurisdiction formerly held by the Court and European Commission of Human Rights (which was abolished). The court is staffed by judges appointed from each of the states party to the Convention, and carries out its work at four different levels. First, a committee of the court consisting of three judges may, by unanimous vote, declare inadmissible an individual application submitted to the court. A complaint is inadmissible if it is "incompatible with the Convention", manifestly ill-founded or an abuse of process. The complainant must have title and interest to complain, must have exhausted all available domestic remedies and must not be time-barred. Decisions of the committee as to admissibility are final. A Chamber consisting of seven judges must decide on the admissibility (if no decision on admissibility has been taken by a committee) and merits of individual applications. The Chamber also has jurisdiction in relation to the admissibility and merits of inter-state applications. The judge representing the "defendant" state must be a member of the Chamber hearing the case against the state. Appeals lie from a decision of a Chamber to the Grand Chamber consisting of 17 judges. A Chamber may choose, furthermore, to relinquish jurisdiction in favour of the Grand Chamber where a case raises a serious question affecting the interpretation of the Convention or where the resolution of the case by the Chamber might conflict with a judgment previously given by the court. Finally, the plenary court is charged with electing the President and Vice-President(s) of the court, setting up the Chambers and electing the Presidents of the Chambers, adopting the rules of the court and electing the Registrar and Deputy Registrar(s).

The first case involving the United Kingdom to reach the court following the grant of the right of individual petition was *Golder v UK* (1975), in which it was held that the refusal by prison authorities to grant a convicted prisoner access to legal advice was in breach of Article 8 and Article 6(1), in that a right of access to legal advice is an aspect of the right to a fair trial. The fight against terrorism in Northern Ireland has accounted for a significant proportion of the cases brought against the United Kingdom, among them *Ireland v UK* (1978), a rare inter-state application concerning breaches of Article 3 by the British security forces in Northern Ireland; *Brogan v United Kingdom* (1988) concerning breaches of Article 5 in the detention of suspected terrorists; and *McCann v UK* (1996), in which it was held that the fatal shooting of three suspected terrorists in Gibraltar was a disproportionate use of lethal force such as to violate Article 2 of the Convention. The United Kingdom was again held in breach of Article 2 in *Jordan v UK* (2001). Considering a number of joined applications, the European Court held that the obligations to protect life read in conjunction with the state's general duty under Article 1 impliedly requires that some form of effective official investigation be made available when individuals are killed as a result of the use of force. Noting that proper procedures for ensuring the accountability of state agents were necessary to maintain public confidence and to meet legitimate concerns that might arise from the use of lethal force—in these cases, that the security forces operated a tacit "shoot to kill" policy in Northern Ireland—the Court found that the investigations conducted in all of the cases were so deficient in transparency and effectiveness as to breach Article 2.

Prior to the entry into force of the Human Rights Act, a number of Scottish cases had made their way to the Commission or Court of Human Rights, including *McMichael v UK* (1995) (which found breaches of Articles 6 and 8 in the conduct of family proceedings) and *Pullar v UK* (1996) (which found no breach of Article 6 in respect of the conduct of a jury trial). Probably the best-known Scottish case to make its way to the court is *Campbell and Cosans v UK* (1982). Two mothers complained that the use of the tawse in Scottish schools was a violation of Article 3, as a form of inhuman or degrading punishment; and of Article 2 of the

First Protocol, which provides that in the provision of education and teaching the state must respect the right of parents to ensure that their children are educated in conformity with their religious and philosophical convictions. The court rejected the first of these arguments but accepted the second on the grounds that "philosophical convictions" include "such convictions as are worthy of respect in a 'democratic society' ... and are not incompatible with human dignity; ... [and which do] not conflict with the fundamental right of the child to education". It was held that the provision of efficient instruction and training and the avoidance of unreasonable expenditure, which the state had pleaded in its defence, was not incompatible with a system of exemption for individual pupils from a system of corporal punishment. In fact, it was provided in the Education (No. 2) Act 1986 that corporal punishment in all state schools in the United Kingdom was to be abolished. In *Costello-Roberts v UK* (1995) the court held that the use of corporal punishment against a seven-year old boy in a private boarding school did not, on the facts, constitute a violation of Article 3. However, in *A v UK* (1998), the state was held to have violated Article 3 in failing to protect a child who was caned by his step-father, following the step-father's successful plea of the defence of "reasonable chastisement" in his prosecution for assault. As both *Costello-Roberts* and *A* imply, the state's obligations under the European Convention are not merely negative in nature (*i.e.* consisting only of an obligation not actively to invade protected rights). In certain circumstances, the court will also be prepared to hold the state subject to positive obligations to prevent violations of protected rights by third parties.

Space precludes a detailed consideration of the cases in which the United Kingdom has been involved, but you might note, among the more important decisions of the court, *Sunday Times v UK* (1979), which held that the law of contempt of court in relation to publications as stated by the House of Lords in *Attorney General v Times Newspapers* (1974) was in breach of Article 10 of the Convention; *Dudgeon v UK* (1981), which held that legislation in Northern Ireland criminalising homosexual activities between consenting adult males was in breach of Article 8; *Malone v UK* (1984), which held that Article 8 had been violated by telephone tapping without positive legal authorisation; and *Observer and Guardian v UK* (1991), which held that the continuance in force of interim injunctions prohibiting press coverage of the allegations of malpractice made in *Spycatcher*, even though the book had been published widely elsewhere in the world, was in breach of Article 10.

Where an adverse judgment is given against it, the United Kingdom comes under an international legal obligation to change national law so as to conform with the Convention (unless it enters a derogation). The approach to compliance has on occasion been somewhat grudging. The provisions of the Contempt of Court Act 1981, enacted in the light of the *Sunday Times* decision, do the bare minimum necessary to achieve compliance; and indeed the United Kingdom was in trouble again in

Goodwin v United Kingdom (1996) in respect of the conviction of a journalist for contempt after he refused to reveal his sources. Similarly, after it was held in *Abdulaziz v United Kingdom* (1985) that British immigration rules discriminated against women contrary to Articles 8 and 14 in that, while the wives and fiancées of men permanently settled in the UK were entitled to enter the UK the husbands and fiancés of women were not, the discrimination was eradicated by removing the entitlement of wives and fiancés to enter: levelling down rather than levelling up.

THE HUMAN RIGHTS ACT

The incorporated rights
Section 1 and Schedule 1 of the Bill specify those Articles of the Convention and the First Protocol which are to be incorporated: Articles 2 to 12, 14, and 16 to 18 of the Convention, Articles 1 to 3 of the First Protocol and Articles 1 and 2 of the Sixth Protocol, concerning the abolition of the death penalty. Thus the duty laid on the state to secure the Convention rights and freedoms under Article 1 and the right to an effective remedy under Article 13 remain enforceable only on the plane of international law.

Interpretation of Convention rights
Section 2 provides that a court or tribunal determining a question in connection with a Convention right must have regard to (although they need not necessarily follow) the relevant judgments, decisions, declarations and opinions of the European Commission and Court of Human Rights and the Committee of Ministers of the Council of Europe. This is an enormous amount of material, and the need to familiarise the courts and tribunals with human rights law largely accounts for the lengthy lapse of time between the passage of the Human Rights Act and its entry into force.

The interpretive obligation
Under section 3 of the Act, all courts and tribunals are required, so far as possible, to read and give effect to legislation, primary or subordinate and whenever passed, consistently with the Convention rights. Prior to the incorporation of the European Convention, the domestic courts would have regard to the Convention rights in interpreting *ambiguous* statutes (on the assumption that Parliament intended to legislate consistently with the international legal obligations of the United Kingdom). The interpretive obligation laid down by section 3 goes much further (although questions remain about quite how far it goes: see *e.g. R v DPP, ex parte Kebilene* (2000); *R v A (No 2)* (2002); *R v Lambert* (2002); *Re S (Care Order: Implementation of Care Plan)* (2002). Only if the legislation is effectively incapable of bearing an interpretation consistent

with the Convention rights are the courts relieved of this strong interpretive duty.

Declarations of incompatibility
In the event that legislation cannot be construed consistently with the Convention rights, certain higher courts have jurisdiction under section 4 of the Act to make a "declaration of incompatibility" in respect of it. For Scotland, those courts are the House of Lords, the Judicial Committee of the Privy Council, the Courts-Martial Appeal Court, the High Court of Justiciary sitting as a court of criminal appeal, and the Court of Session. It is expressly provided that a declaration of incompatibility will have no effect on the validity, continuing operation or enforcement of the provision in respect of which it is given; nor is it binding on the parties to the proceedings in which it is made. For this reason, a declaration of incompatibility is scarcely to be seen as a desirable remedy. Litigants will prefer to join battle on the correct interpretation of legislation with a view to securing a concrete remedy, such as interdict or damages.

The language of section 4 preserves, at least in appearance, parliamentary supremacy. Theoretically, it will remain open to Parliament to ignore a declaration of incompatibility, and such a declaration is *not* to be regarded as a binding decision that the Act of Parliament in question is *ultra vires* and invalid. However, section 10 of the Act lays down powers to take "remedial action". If a provision of legislation has been declared to be incompatible with Convention rights, or if it appears to a minister of the Crown or Her Majesty in Council that, in the light of a finding of the European Court of Human Rights, a provision of legislation is incompatible with obligations of the United Kingdom arising from the Convention, the minister may by order make such amendments to the legislation (including its repeal) as he considers appropriate. Such a remedial order must be approved in draft by resolution of each House of Parliament except where urgency requires that the order is made without a draft being approved, in which case this must be stated expressly in the order and the order must be laid before Parliament after it is made. Each House must approve the order within 40 days or it will cease to have effect.

There are parallels to be drawn here between the Human Rights Act and the Scotland Act, both of which stress that the legislative supremacy of the Westminster Parliament is unaffected by their provisions. It would appear that the object of the government was to achieve far-reaching measures of constitutional reform while keeping faith with the British constitutional tradition, of which parliamentary supremacy is very much a part. Note, however, one salient distinction between Acts of the Westminster Parliament and Acts of the Scottish Parliament: where the former are incompatible with the Convention rights, they may be subject to declarations of incompatibility; the latter are liable to be struck down as invalid. A parallel may also be drawn between the power conferred on the courts by the Human Rights Act to make declarations of incompatibility with the role of the courts in relation to Community law. We have seen that the courts will declare an Act of Parliament to be incompatible with Community law (*R v Transport Secretary, ex parte Factortame (No. 2)* (1991); *R v Employment Secretary, ex parte Equal Opportunities Commission* (1995)). What the courts do *not* do, however, is hold such an Act to be *ultra vires* and void for incompatibility with Community law. Their language is of "compatibility" rather than "validity"—consciously so—and to that extent their judgments have an advisory rather than dispositive flavour. Thus it falls to Parliament to correct the incompatibility that the courts have declared if it sees fit to do so, and although in practice it has always done so, this approach preserves at least a veneer of legal truth in the notion that Parliament can make or unmake any law whatever and no court may set aside an Act of Parliament.

Public authorities

Section 6(1) provides that "it is unlawful for a public authority to act in a way which is incompatible with a Convention right". Public authorities are therefore under a general duty in the exercise of their powers and the discharge of their duties to respect Convention rights—regardless of whether the question ever comes before a court. This general principle is to some extent qualified by the terms of section 6(2) of the Act, which states that a public authority shall *not* be held to have acted unlawfully (that is, in breach of Convention rights) if, because of the terms of its enabling legislation, it could not have acted in any other way. In other words, wherever a public authority exercises a statutory power or performs a statutory duty that contains an element of discretion, that discretion must be exercised in a manner consistent with the Convention rights. It is only where a public authority has *no* discretion that the simple performance of statutory functions may override the observance of Convention rights, and such situations will be relatively rare.

The term "public authority" is defined to include a court or tribunal (section 6(3)(a)) and "any person certain of whose functions are functions of a public nature" (section 6(3)(b)), but *not* either House of Parliament, other than the House of Lords in its judicial capacity, or anyone exercising functions in connection with proceedings in Parliament. It follows from section 6(3)(b) that a body may qualify as a "public authority" for the purposes of the Human Rights Act, provided it performs public functions, even if it is not obviously a public authority in terms of its legal constitution. However, section 6(5) states that "in relation to a particular act, a person is not a public authority by virtue *only* of section 6(3)(b) if the nature of the act is private". In other words, as the Home Secretary explained during the passage through Parliament of the Human Rights Bill, while certain classic or "obvious" public authorities such as local authorities, government departments, the police and the armed forces are bound to act in conformity with the Convention rights across the board, other bodies are only bound so far as they are performing public functions. Beyond that, their position is the same as that of a wholly private entity or person: they are not caught by the duty contained in section 6(1). However, the "public function" test, while easy to state, has been less easy to apply in practice (see, *e.g. Poplar Housing and Regeneration Community Association Ltd v Donoghue* (2002); *R (Heather) v Leonard Cheshire Foundation* (2002)).

None of this is to say that the Human Rights Act is altogether without impact in purely private relationships and contexts. On the contrary, there is scope for the Human Rights Act to have "horizontal effect" on two grounds. First, in the application of legislation to private relationships—such as the application of employment protection legislation to employment relationships—the courts are required by section 3 of the Human Rights Act to read and give effect to that legislation consistently with the Convention rights regardless of the character of the parties before them. Equally, if it is not possible to read a provision of legislation in such a way, the court is entitled even in proceedings between private parties to make a declaration of incompatibility in respect of it, as the English Court of Appeal held in relation to a provision of the Consumer Credit Act 1974 in *Wilson v First County Trust Ltd (No 2)* (2001) (although the declaration of incompatibility was subsequently overturned by the House of Lords, which found no breach of the Convention rights). Secondly, where the court is applying common law doctrines or making decisions about remedies or procedure, its duty under section 6 of the Human Rights Act obliges it to act in conformity with Convention rights in a dispute between private parties as much as in one involving a public authority (see, *e.g. Douglas v Hello! Magazine Ltd (No 2)* (2003); *Karl Construction Ltd v Palisade Properties Ltd* (2002)). Thus even while section 6 only applies to classic public authorities or to "hybrid" bodies so far as they are carrying out public functions, the potential for the indirect effect of the Human Rights Act should not be underestimated.

Proceedings under the Human Rights Act

Under section 7 of the Act, a person who claims that a public authority has acted or proposes to act in a way which is unlawful by virtue of section 6 may, if and only if he is or would be a victim of such unlawful act, bring proceedings against the authority in the appropriate court or tribunal or rely on the Convention right or rights concerned in any legal proceedings. The court or tribunal seised of such a dispute may "grant such relief or remedy, or make such order, within its jurisdiction as it considers just and appropriate", including damages. Damages may only be awarded, however, by a court which has power to award damages or to order payment of compensation in civil proceedings, and no award of damages may be made unless the court is satisfied, having regard to all the circumstances, that the award is necessary to afford "just satisfaction" to the person in whose favour it is made.

---

10. POLICE POWERS

ARREST

An arrest may be effected with or without a warrant, under statute or at common law, but almost all arrests are made by police officers. The power of ordinary people to effect a "citizen's arrest" is strictly circumscribed in Scotland. "A private citizen is entitled to arrest without warrant for a serious crime he has witnessed, or where he has a moral certainty that the person he arrests has just committed a crime or perhaps where, being the victim of the crime, he has information equivalent to personal observation, as where the fleeing criminal is pointed out to him by an eyewitness": see *e.g. Codona v Cardle* (1989); *Bryans v Guild* (1990); *Lees v Wightman* (2000). Beyond this, a private citizen who purports to arrest a person may render himself liable to conviction for assault.

The meaning of arrest was considered in *Forbes v HM Advocate* (1990). For an arrest to be lawful, the High Court of Justiciary stressed that the police should make clear to the arrestee that he was under legal compulsion and should tell him the (correct) reason for his arrest. It is preferable to use the word "arrest" here, but "any form of words will suffice to inform the person that he is being arrested if they bring to his notice the fact that he is under compulsion and the person thereafter submits to that compulsion" *per* Lord Parker CJ, *Alderson v Booth* (1969). Reasonable physical force may be used to effect an arrest, and it is an offence under section 41, Police (Scotland) Act 1967 to resist a lawful arrest or to escape from lawful custody.

A person who has been arrested and is in custody has the right under section 15(1), Criminal Procedure (Scotland) Act 1995, to have intimation of his custody and of the place where he is being held sent to a third party without delay, or with no more delay than is necessary in the interest of the investigation or prevention of crime or the apprehension of offenders. He must be informed of this entitlement on arrival at the police station. Under section 17(1) of the 1995 Act, he is also entitled to request the attendance of a solicitor at the place where he is being held; again, he must be informed of this right.

Police powers of arrest fall into three categories: arrest with a warrant; arrest without warrant under statutory provisions; and arrest without warrant at common law.

Arrest with a warrant

When an arrest is deemed necessary (because there is sufficient evidence to bring charges), the procurator fiscal will present a petition to the sheriff court or district court seeking the power to arrest the suspect and bring him before the court (along with other powers such as a power to search the suspect and his property). The sheriff or justice is entitled to grant the warrant without close inquiry into the grounds on which it is sought, if he has sworn information that there are reasonable grounds for suspicion. The validity of a warrant may be challenged by way of a bill of suspension in the High Court (*Stuart v Crowe* (1992)) or, after the trial and in the event of the accused being convicted, by way of a bill or petition to the *nobile officium* of the High Court. A warrant which is valid on its face cannot, however, be challenged in the course of a trial before the sheriff (*Allan v Tant* (1986)).

Arrest without warrant under statute

A great many statutes confer a power of arrest without warrant on a police constable (usually "in uniform") where certain specified conditions are satisfied. The courts normally require fairly strict compliance by the police with the terms of a statutory power of arrest. In *Wither v Reid* (1980), the accused was charged with an offence under section 41, Police (Scotland) Act 1967 after she resisted a clothing and body search for drugs (none were found), having been arrested under section 24(1), Misuse of Drugs Act 1971. Section 24 provides that a constable may arrest without warrant a person whom he reasonably suspects of having committed an offence under the Act if he has reasonable cause to believe that the person will abscond unless arrested, or if he does not know and cannot ascertain the name and address of the person, or if he believes that the name and address given are false. The accused was arrested at Elgin station by police who had received information from her estranged ex-fiancé that she had been to Aberdeen to buy drugs. The sheriff acquitted the accused, holding that there was nothing to justify her arrest under any of the provisions of section 24 and that, as her arrest was illegal, she was entitled to resist the consequently unlawful search. The High Court, by a majority, dismissed the procurator fiscal's appeal.

Note, however, that where, as is usual, a statutory provision makes a power of arrest conditional upon a "reasonable belief" on the part of the arresting officer that an offence has been committed by the arrestee, the courts do not inquire too closely into the reasonableness of the officer's belief or suspicion. It was held in *McLeod v Shaw* (1981) that the test is subjective; provided the arresting officer honestly believed that the arrestee was committing or had committed the relevant offence, the arrest is valid and lawful unless the officer could have had no reasonable grounds at all for that belief. It is questionable whether this approach is compatible with Article 5 of the ECHR, which requires reasonable grounds, objectively judged, for suspicion that a person has committed a criminal offence by way of justification for arrest.

Arrest without warrant at common law

It was established in *Peggie v Clark* (1868) that a constable may at common law arrest without warrant a person whom he reasonably believes to have committed an offence, in order "to prevent justice from being defeated", *per* Lord Deas.

This translates into a formidably broad power of arrest. Bear in mind that:

- As with arrest without warrant under statute, the reasonableness of the arresting officer's belief that a crime has been committed by the arrestee is assessed subjectively Only if, as in *Cardle v Murray* (1993), there are no reasonable grounds to support the officer's honest belief will an arrest be unlawful. Similar considerations regarding the compatibility of this position with Article 5 of the ECHR therefore arise.
- The arrest must be necessary in the interests of justice, as Lord Deas indicated in *Peggie*. It is not enough that an offence has been committed. The arresting officer must also believe, *e.g.* that the person will abscond unless arrested, or will otherwise interfere with the course of justice. Urgency may justify an arrest in the interests of justice; by the same token, the longer the lapse of time since the commission of an offence, the less easy it will be to justify arrest without warrant.
- The more serious the offence concerned, the easier it is to justify arrest without warrant at common law (but note that a constable may arrest without warrant a person who is committing, or who leads the constable reasonably to apprehend, a breach of the peace (*Montgomery v McLeod* (1977)).

In general terms, as the Lord President put it in *Peggie*, "under special circumstances, a police officer is entitled to apprehend without a warrant, and it will always be a question whether the circumstances justify the apprehension". The only caveat to this proposition is that the circumstances might not need to be so distinctively "special" as the Lord President perhaps implied.

DETENTION

Statutory powers of "quasi-detention" and detention are now contained in sections 13 and 14, Criminal Procedure (Scotland) Act 1995.

Section 13(1)(a) provides that where a constable has reasonable grounds for suspecting that a person has committed or is committing an offence at any place, he may require that person to give his name and address and may ask him for an explanation of the circumstances which have given rise to the constable's suspicion. The constable may require that person to remain with him while he verifies the name and address and/or notes the explanation offered, provided that this can be done quickly, and may use reasonable force to ensure that the person remains with him. The constable must inform the person of his suspicion and of the general nature of the offence which he suspects the person has committed or is committing, and if necessary must inform the person why he is being required to remain with him. He must also inform the person that failure to comply with his requirements may constitute an offence for which he may be arrested without warrant.

Under section 13(1)(b), a constable may also require any other person whom he believes to have information relating to the offence to give his name and address. He must inform that person of the general nature of the offence which he suspects has been or is being committed, and that the reason for the requirement is that he believes the person has relevant information. A person who fails to give his name and address without reasonable excuse is guilty of an offence.

Section 14(1) provides that, where a constable has reasonable grounds for suspecting that a person has committed or is committing an offence punishable by imprisonment, he may, for the purpose of facilitating the carrying out of investigations into the offence and as to whether criminal proceedings should be instigated against the person, detain that person. Reasonable force may be used. Where a person is detained, the constable may exercise the same powers of search as are available following arrest (see below); again, reasonable force may be used. The detainee must be taken as quickly as is reasonably practicable to a police station or other premises, and may thereafter be taken elsewhere.

Detention must be terminated at the end of six hours, and sooner if it appears that there are no longer grounds for detention or if the detainee is arrested or detained pursuant to another statutory provision. Where a person is released at the termination of a period of detention under section 14(1) he cannot be re-detained under the subsection on the same grounds or on any grounds arising out of the same circumstances. Where a person has previously been detained pursuant to another statutory provision, and is then detained under section 14(1) on the same grounds or on any grounds arising from the same circumstances, the six-hour detention period must be reduced by the length of his earlier detention.

A constable who detains a person under section 14(1) must inform the person of his suspicion, of the general nature of the offence which he suspects has been or is being committed, and of the reason for the detention. A number of matters require to be recorded by the police:

- The place where detention begins and the police station or other premises to which the detainee is taken.
- The general nature of the suspected offence.

- The time when detention begins and the time of the detainee's arrival at the police station or other premises.
- The time of the detainee's release from detention or, as the case may be, the time of his arrest.
- That the detainee has been informed of his right, both at the moment of detention and again on arrival at the police station, to refuse to answer any question other than to give his name and address (this is the statutory caution).
- That the detainee has been informed of his rights under section 15(1)(b) of the 1995 Act, namely the right to have intimation of his detention and of the place where he is being held sent to a solicitor and to one other person reasonably named by him (*e.g.* a friend or relative) without delay, or with no more delay than is necessary in the interest of the investigation or prevention of crime or the apprehension of offenders.
- Where the detainee exercises his rights under section 15(1)(b), the time at which his request is made and the time at which it is complied with.
- The identity of the constable who informs the detainee of his rights.

An initial point to make about these provisions is that the status of a person required to "remain" under section 13 while a constable checks his name and address and/or notes his explanation is unclear. While the section must mean something less than detention (otherwise there would be no need for section 13 at all), note that a person may not only be required to remain but can be physically constrained to do so. Moreover, while the constable has the power to require an explanation of the circumstances which have given rise to his suspicion, he is not enjoined to administer a caution at this stage. Presumably if the circumstances were such that a constable felt a caution to be appropriate, the section 14 power to detain should be used instead. However, the line between sections 13 and 14—or the line between the situations in which one power or the other is appropriate—is not clear, and it is likely that any explanation offered by a person asked to remain under section 13 would be admissible at a subsequent trial subject to the normal rules of evidence.

So far as detention proper is concerned, it must be stressed that detention is not to be used as a means of delaying arrest and charge. If sufficient evidence emerges to justify arrest of a detainee, detention must be terminated and must in any event be terminated after six hours. Note, however, that in *Grant v H.M. Advocate* (1990) the accused was not arrested until some 20 minutes after the end of his detention, and objection was taken at his trial to the admissibility in evidence of statements he had made while detained. The High Court held that such lapses in compliance with the strict formalities did not of themselves vitiate what had taken place.

A statutory caution must be administered to the detainee, both at the time of detention and again on arrival at the place of detention. Section

14(7)(a) provides that the power to question a detainee is without prejudice to any relevant rule of law regarding the admissibility in evidence of any answer given. The common law applies a test of fairness to determine issues of admissibility, and it was held in *Tonge, Grey and Jack v H.M. Advocate* (1982) that a full common law caution should also be administered to a detainee prior to questioning if the evidence thus obtained is to avoid the risk of being held inadmissible because obtained unfairly. Failure to administer the statutory caution is less likely to be fatal to a subsequent prosecution. In *Scott v Howie* (1993), the accused was detained and taken to the police station. The statutory caution was not given at the moment of detention, but at the commencement of questioning both the statutory caution and a full common law caution were given. The accused then made a statement, which the Crown founded upon at his trial. The High Court held that what had occurred was a procedural defect which did not vitiate the admissibility in evidence of the accused statement, the statement being open to no objection when measured by the common law test of fairness. Any statements made by the accused between the commencement of his detention and his arrival at the police station would, however, have been inadmissible.

Once detained, the detainee must be removed to a police station or other premises, and during detention he may be removed elsewhere (*e.g.* to take part in an identification parade). In *Menzies v H.M. Advocate* (1995), the accused was detained near Airdrie and taken to Dunfermline police station, since the interviewing facilities at Airdrie were busy and all the documentation relating to the offence with which the accused was eventually charged was in Dunfermline. The High Court held that the requirement that the detainee be taken away "as quickly as is reasonably practicable" did not mean that he had to be taken to the nearest police station. The requirement was conditional upon what was reasonably practicable in the circumstances as they appeared to the constable by whom the person was detained.

The requirement of recording the details of detention should as a matter of good police practice be adhered to, although it is arguable that failure to record a particular detail will not render the detention unlawful and statements made by the detainee inadmissible. In *Cummings v H.M. Advocate* (1982), the only record led in evidence to show that the accused had received a statutory caution was contained in a police officer's notebook. This was held to be sufficient.

SEARCH

Search of persons
First, a person may be searched with his or her consent (*Devlin v Normand* (1992)). At common law, a person may be searched (and fingerprinted and photographed) by the police only after arrest, although in situations of "urgency" searches carried out before arrest may be

excused and the evidence obtained admitted at trial (*Bell v Hogg* (1967)). Search before arrest must be justified by reference to some statutory provision, *e.g.* section 23(2), Misuse of Drugs Act 1971, whereby a constable who has reasonable grounds to suspect that a person is in possession of drugs may detain and search him. On the principle of *Wither v Reid* (1980), the courts will normally require the police to comply closely with the terms of statutory powers of search.

When a person has been arrested and is in custody, or where he has been detained under section 14, Criminal Procedure (Scotland) Act 1995, section 18(2) of that Act provides that a constable may take from that person fingerprints, palm prints and other such prints and impressions of an external part of the body as the constable reasonably considers it appropriate to take, having regard to the circumstances of the suspected offence in respect of which the person has been arrested or detained. Section 18(6) provides that the constable may also take, with the authority of an officer of a rank no lower than inspector, a sample of hair; a sample of fingernail or toenail (or of material under the nails); a sample of blood or other body fluid, body tissue or other material from an external part of the body by means of swabbing or rubbing; or a sample of saliva. Reasonable force may be used. Section 58 of the Criminal Justice (Scotland) Act 1995 further provides that swabs may be taken from the mouth for the purpose of DNA fingerprinting.

If a sample is sought before arrest or detention, or if samples not covered by the statutory provisions (*e.g.* dental impressions: *Hay v HM Advocate* (1968)) are required, then the procurator fiscal must seek the authority of a sheriff's warrant. It was held in *Morris v MacNeill* (1991) that "such a warrant will not be lightly granted, and will only be granted where the circumstances are special and where the granting of the warrant will not disturb the delicate balance that must be maintained between the public interest on the one hand and the interest of the accused on the other". However, it does not appear to require much for the circumstances to be sufficiently special. One factor taken into account here is the seriousness of the offence, yet in *Walker v Lees* (1995) a warrant was granted to take blood samples from a person suspected of theft from lockfast cars. If the Crown can show that the samples sought will provide useful evidence, they are likely to get the warrant craved: the unusual cases will be those in which the warrant is refused.

Search of premises

It was established in *Bell v Black and Morrison* (1865) that a general warrant to search any premises for any articles is incompetent. A search warrant must be specific in its terms and the police must keep within the limits of a warrant when conducting a search under it: a police officer authorised by warrant to search for article X may not actively look for article Y. As this implies, the officers who conduct a search must be aware of the specifications of the warrant. The officers were not so aware in *Leckie v Miln* (1981). In their search of the suspect's house, they removed a number of articles which were outside the terms of the warrant. These articles were held by the High Court to have been unlawfully obtained. They were therefore inadmissible in evidence against the accused and his conviction for theft was quashed. Nor did it matter that the police had been given permission to search the house by the suspect's wife: any permission must be treated as limited to a search conducted within the terms of the warrant.

It often happens, however, that police officers engaged on a lawful search of premises stumble across articles not covered by the warrant. Can such articles lawfully be removed, and will they be admissible in evidence? In *HM Advocate v Hepper* (1958), Lord Guthrie held that "the police officers were not prevented from taking possession of other articles of a plainly incriminatory character which they happened to come across in the course of their search." In *Drummond v HM Advocate* (1992), the accused was charged with the theft of clothes. Some of the clothes had been found in a wardrobe at his home as it was searched by two police officers executing a warrant relating to stolen furniture. When the first constable was asked what he was looking for in the wardrobe, he admitted that he was looking for "stuff" from the clothing theft. The sheriff ruled his evidence inadmissible. The second constable, however, said that he had a list of the stolen furniture which included small items such as lamps, and that he was looking for these items in the wardrobe when the stolen clothing attracted his attention. The sheriff allowed the evidence of the second constable to go to the jury, which convicted the accused.

At common law, the power of the police to enter and search private premises is limited. As a starting point, it may be said that the right of a police officer to enter private premises for any purpose without a warrant and without the occupier's consent is no greater than that of any other member of the public; and if the police do so enter, they must be prepared to justify their conduct by reference to special circumstances before any evidence thus obtained may be held admissible (*Cairns v Keane* (1983)). As the Lord Justice-General put it in *Lawrie v Muir* (1950):

> "Irregularities require to be excused, and infringements of the formalities of the law in relation to these matters are not lightly to be condoned. Whether any given irregularity ought to be excused depends upon the nature of the irregularity and the circumstances under which it was committed."

An urgent need to obtain evidence, particularly in relation to serious offences, may justify a search without warrant of private property (*H.M. Advocate v McGuigan* (1936)). Other circumstances which may excuse an irrregular search are the authority and good faith of those who obtained the evidence. In *Lawrie v Muir*, one ground upon which the High Court quashed the conviction was that the evidence had been obtained from the accused's dairy not by police officers but by two inspectors who should have known "the precise limits of their authority and should be held to exceed these limits at their peril". Similarly, in relation to search of a person rather than search of premises, it was held in *Wilson v Brown* (1996) that stewards employed at a nightclub in Ayr could legitimately have detained the accused until the police arrived, but that they had no authority whatsoever to search him (finding, in the process, 78 temazepam capsules) and that the circumstances were not such as to excuse the irregularity of the search. Good faith was a factor in *Webley v Ritchie* (1997). The accused was convicted of the theft of three squash racquets. While he was in detention in connection with the theft, two police officers located his car, forced it open and found the stolen racquets in the boot. The racquets were held to be admissible in evidence at his trial, not only because the police had acted reasonably and in good faith in forcing open the car, but also because, as there was a risk that the six-hour detention period would expire before a warrant could be obtained, there was an urgent need to search the car in order to preserve any evidence. The offence, however, can hardly be described as "serious".

Overarching all of these factors is the general principle governing the admissibility of evidence, namely the test of fairness. This is considered further in the next section.

QUESTIONING

Once a person has been formally charged, he cannot be questioned further about the offence with which he has been charged (*Carmichael v Boyd* (1993)). But there is no general rule that the police cannot question a person after he has been arrested, provided the questioning is not unfair (*Johnston v H.M. Advocate* (1993)), and of course questioning is often the very point of detention under section 14, Criminal Procedure (Scotland) Act 1995.

An important aspect of the fairness of questioning, and hence of the admissibility in evidence of statements made in response, is cautioning the person being questioned. We have seen, in the context of detention, that the police should administer a statutory caution to the detainee both at the moment of detention and again on arrival at the police station; and a full common law caution should also be given prior to questioning a detainee (*Tonge, Grey and Jack v H.M. Advocate* (1982)). To avoid any risk of rendering statements inadmissible, a common law caution should be administered at the outset of any form of questioning, and re-administered as often as necessary during a long period of questioning: the suspect should be told that he is not obliged to say anything, but that anything he does say will be taken down (and tape-recorded) and may be used in evidence. But there is no absolute rule that a caution must always be given. In *Pennycuick v Lees* (1992), where the accused was charged with benefits fraud, objection was taken to the admissibility of incriminating statements made by the accused in response to questions from social security investigators on the grounds that the investigators had failed to caution him. The Lord Justice-General held:

> "There is ... no rule of law which requires that a suspect must always be cautioned before any question can be put to him by the police or by anyone else by whom the inquiries are being conducted. The question in each case is whether what was done was unfair to the accused ... [I]t is important to note that there is no suggestion in [this] case that any undue pressure, deception or other device was used to obtain the admissions."

In *Young v Friel* (1992) it was argued unsuccessfully that the police officer had unfairly induced the accused to make self-incriminating statements when he told the accused that "I can't offer you any deals at present". However, in *H.M. Advocate v Graham* (1991) it was held that incriminating statements made by the accused to a business colleague and secretly recorded by the police with the colleague's knowledge were inadmissible in evidence. In short, then, failure to caution is not fatal to the admissibility of statements given in response to questioning, provided that there is no suggestion of inducement, entrapment, deception, pressure or anything else apt to render the questioning unfair.

A trial judge will normally be justified in withholding the evidence of statements from the jury only if he is satisfied that no reasonable jury could hold that the evidence had not been extracted from the suspect by unfair or improper means—only if, in other words, "it is abundantly clear that the rules of fairness and fair dealing have been flagrantly transgressed" (*per* Lord Cameron, *HM Advocate v Whitelaw* (1980), and see also *Lord Advocate's Reference (No. 1 of 1983)* (1984)). But what exactly the rules of fairness require is not necessarily easy to pin down. A position relatively favourable to the accused was adopted in *Chalmers v H.M. Advocate* (1954). The Lord Justice-General held:

> "[B]y our law, self-incriminating statements when tendered in evidence at a criminal trial, are always jealously examined from the standpoint of being assured as to their spontaneity; and if, on a review of all the proved circumstances, that test is not satisfied, evidence of such statements will usually be excluded altogether."

Subsequently, in *Miln v Cullen* (1967), the High Court shifted the emphasis of the test of fairness further in the direction of the public interest in the detection and prosecution of crime. The Lord Justice-Clerk observed that:

> "While, according to our common law, no man is bound to incriminate himself, there is, in general, nothing to prevent a man making a voluntary and incriminating statement to the police if he so chooses, and evidence being led of that statement at his subsequent trial on the charge to which the statement relates ... [In this case] there was no interrogation in the proper sense of that word, no

extraction of a confession by cross-examination, no taint of undue pressure, cajoling or trapping, no bullying and nothing in the nature of third degree, and it is not suggested that the respondent, by reason of low intelligence, immaturity or drink, was incapable of appreciating what was going on."

More recent cases, however, may indicate a shift back towards *Chalmers*. In *Black v Annan* (1995) Lord Sutherland held that:

"If the question of impropriety is raised, it lies with the Crown to establish that any statement was in fact voluntarily made and that there was no unfairness in the extraction of that statement. It is not a matter of the accused having to establish that there was sufficient impropriety to justify the extraction of the statement made by him."

In *Codona v HMA* (1996), a 14-year old girl had been convicted along with three young men of murder. Her conviction was quashed on the grounds that the evidence of her statements in response to police questioning should not have been allowed to go to the jury. The questioning had taken place over some three and a half hours and was of such a character as to demonstrate an intention to extract admissions which the girl was unwilling to make voluntarily. This, coupled with the girl's age and vulnerability (her damaging admissions were only made at a late stage of the questioning, after she had begun to cry), was sufficient to render what had happened unfair. But *Codona* should not necessarily be taken as confined to its special circumstances. In general terms, the Lord Justice-General held that:

"[I]n order that a statement made by an accused person to the police may be available as evidence against him, it must be truly spontaneous and voluntary. The police may question a suspect, but when they move into the field of cross-examination or interrogation, they move into an area of great difficulty. If the questioning is carried too far, by means of leading or repetitive questioning or by pressure in other ways in an effort to obtain from the suspect what they are seeking to obtain from him, the statement is likely to be excluded on the ground that it was extracted by unfair means. Lord Justice-General Emslie's definition of the words 'interrogation' and 'cross-examination' in *Lord Advocate's Reference (No. 1 of 1983)*, as referring only to improper forms of questioning tainted with an element of bullying or pressure designed to break the will of the suspect or to force from him a confession against his will, should not be understood as implying any weakening of these important principles."

Although, as Sheriff Gordon remarks in his commentary on *Codona*, the issue of whether police questioning "degenerated into unacceptable pressure might be regarded as quintessentially one for the jury", the stricter the test of fairness then the easier it is for a trial judge to justify withholding evidence from the jury on the basis that no reasonable jury could conclude that it had been fairly obtained. It is also safe to say that the stricter approach is less likely to require re-assessment in the light of the entry into force of the Human Rights Act. As to that, it has been held that although the right to a fair trial under Article 6 of the ECHR is an absolute right in the sense that a conviction obtained unfairly cannot stand, the elements of a fair trial—such as the presumption of innocence—are not absolute requirements and may be restricted if necessary for the achievement of legitimate aims and provided there is a reasonable relationship of proportionality between the means employed and the aim to be realised (see *e.g. Brown v Stott* (2001)). The overarching question under the Convention as at common law is whether the trial viewed as a whole is fair. That is a matter not merely of the fairness of admitting particular items of evidence, but extends to all the other incidents of a fair trial, such as the right to be tried within a reasonable time (*Dyer v Watson* (2002)), the right to an independent and impartial tribunal (*Starrs v Ruxton* (2000)) and the right to equality of arms as between prosecution and defence.

11. PUBLIC ORDER

Prior to the entry into force of the Human Rights Act 1998, there was no legal right to assemble, protest and demonstrate. Rather, as Lord Dunedin put it in *McAra v Magistrates of Edinburgh* (1913), "you may say what you like ... but that does not mean you may say it anywhere". "Freedom of expression and assembly", which are enshrined in Articles 10 and 11 of the ECHR respectively, therefore denoted the limited space left by common law and statutory restrictions imposed in the interest of maintaining and enforcing public order.

The significance of the 1998 Act is not confined to the fact that it creates legally enforceable rights of free expression and assembly. Under section 6(1) of the Act, a public authority cannot lawfully act in a manner incompatible with the Convention rights. Thus where police officers or local authorities exercise their statutory powers in the field of public order, they must do so consistently with the Convention rights unless the statutory provision in question simply does not admit of a compatible interpretation. In that event, the public authority has a "defence" under section 6(2) and the only remedy remaining for the aggrieved individual will be a declaration of incompatibility under section 4 of the Act (unless the relevant statutory provision is contained in an Act of the Scottish

Parliament, in which case it may simply be struck down). The duty of public authorities under section 6 is reinforced by the duty laid on the courts by section 3 of the Act to read and give effect to legislation, so far as possible, in a manner compatible with the Convention rights. Moreover, being themselves "public authorities" for the purposes of section 6, the courts are obliged to apply and develop the common law consistently with the Convention rights.

Comparatively few cases on freedom of assembly under Article 11 have been considered by the European Court of Human Rights. Most public order cases are disposed of under Article 10 instead (see *e.g. Steel v United Kingdom* (1999) and *Hashman and Harrup v United Kingdom* (1999)). The leading Article 11 cases, *Christians against Racism and Fascism v United Kingdom* (1980) and *Plattform "Ärtze für das Leben" v Austria* (1988), have concerned public demonstrations, although it is clear that the right obtains in relation both to public and private assemblies. It is a right to peaceful assembly only, and cannot be claimed by those bent on violence. The right also has a positive dimension, in the sense that the liability of the state for breach of Article 11 may be engaged when it fails to prevent others, such as violent counter-demonstrators, from interfering with the enjoyment of the right.

Both freedom of assembly and freedom of expression may be restricted, provided that restrictions are "prescribed by law" and necessary in a democratic society in the interests of, *inter alia*, the prevention of disorder or crime. Any such restriction must also be shown to be a proportionate response to the threat to the public interest.

STATUTORY CONTROLS ON PUBLIC PROCESSIONS

Section 62, Civic Government (Scotland) Act 1982 lays down a general requirement of advance notification of public processions. Note, however, that:

- Advance notification is not required for processions which are "customarily or commonly held", unless the local authority has disapplied this exemption from certain customary processions.
- The local authority may waive the full period of notice but not the requirement of notification as such in respect of processions which are spontaneous or organised urgently in response to a particular event and which cannot therefore be notified in advance in accordance with section 62.

In general, then, the organisers of a public procession must give the relevant local authority and chief constable at least seven days' notice of the procession. Under section 63 of the 1982 Act, the council may, after consulting the chief constable, issue an order either prohibiting the procession or imposing upon it conditions as to its date, time, duration and route. The council may also prohibit entry by the procession into any public place specified in the order. The order must be issued in writing at least two days before the procession is, or was to be, held.

Under section 64, appeals lie to the sheriff against an order made under section 63 within 14 days of receipt of the order. The sheriff may only uphold an appeal if he considers that the council in arriving at its decision to make the order erred in law, based itself on a material error of fact, exercised its discretion unreasonably (in the *Wednesbury* sense) or otherwise acted beyond its powers.

Section 65 provides that it is an offence to hold a procession without giving notice as required by section 62 or in contravention of the terms of an order made under section 63. A person who takes part in such a procession and who refuses to desist when required to do so by a uniformed police officer is also guilty of an offence.

The 1982 Act only provided for advance control of processions by local authorities. It did not confer on the police powers to impose conditions, which powers may have proved necessary in the event of unforeseen developments during a march. Section 12 of the Public Order Act 1986 was therefore extended to Scotland. Under this provision, the senior police officer present at the scene of any public procession may impose conditions as to time, place and manner where, having regard to the time, place, circumstances and route in or on which any public procession is being held, he reasonably believes that it may lead to serious public disorder, serious damage to property or serious disruption of the life of the community; or that the purpose of the organisers is to intimidate others with a view to preventing them doing what they have a right to do or compelling them to do something that they have no right to do. The conditions imposed must be those that the police officer believes to be necessary to prevent serious disorder, damage to property, disruption or intimidation. The senior police officer may likewise impose conditions in advance of a procession, but only where people are assembling with a view to taking part in it. The "senior police officer" is the officer most senior in rank present at the scene. Under section 12(4) and (5) it is an offence knowingly to fail to comply with conditions imposed under this section, although it is a defence to prove that the failure arose from circumstances beyond one's control. It is also an offence under section 12(6) to incite others to commit an offence under this section.

STATUTORY CONTROLS ON PUBLIC ASSEMBLIES

Powers to regulate and control public assemblies are conferred directly upon the police by section 14, Public Order Act 1986. If the senior police officer, having regard to the time, place and circumstances in which any public assembly is being or is intended to be held, reasonably believes that it may lead to serious public disorder, serious damage to property or serious disruption of the life of the community, or that the purpose of the organisers is intimidatory in the sense described above, he may give directions imposing on the organisers and participants such conditions as to the venue, duration and maximum number of persons who may take part as appear necessary to prevent such serious disorder, damage or disruption.

These powers apply to a "public assembly", which is defined by section 16 of the Act as meaning "an assembly of 20 or more persons in a public place which is wholly or partly open to the air". "Public place" means "any road within the meaning of the Roads (Scotland) Act 1984" and "any place to which at the material time the public or any section of the public has access, on payment or otherwise, as of right or by virtue of express or implied permission". Where an assembly is in progress, the "senior police officer" is the officer most senior in rank present at the scene. Where an assembly has been proposed, it is the chief officer of police, whose directions must be issued in writing.

A person who organises or takes part in such an assembly and who knowingly fails to comply with such directions is guilty of an offence (section 14(4) and (5)) although it is a defence in either case to prove that failure to comply was due to circumstances beyond one's control. It is also an offence to incite others to commit an offence under this section (section 14(6)).

These powers are clearly limited by the wording of the statute: the police cannot impose conditions on either processions or assemblies unless serious consequences are anticipated. But these powers are not to be taken in isolation. Moreover, the statutory powers of the police in relation to assemblies were augmented by the Criminal Justice and Public Order Act 1994. Section 70 of that Act inserted new sections 14A and 14B into the Public Order Act 1986. Section 14A prohibits "trespassory assemblies", meaning an assembly of 20 or more persons on land wholly in the open air to which the public has no or only limited right of access. If at any time the chief officer of police reasonably believes that a trespassory assembly is intended to be held and that it is likely to cause serious disruption to the life of the community or significant damage to the land or a building or monument on it (where the land, building or monument are of historical, architectural, archaeological or scientific importance), he may apply to the local authority for an order prohibiting for a specified period not exceeding four days all trespassory assemblies in an area not exceeding the area represented by a circle with a radius of five miles from a specified centre. Section 14B prescribes the offences in connection with trespassory assemblies. A person who organises or takes part in an assembly which he knows to be prohibited by an order made under section 14A is guilty of an offence. A person who incites others to take part in a prohibited assembly is also guilty of an offence. Under section 14C, a uniformed police officer may stop a person whom he reasonably believes to be on his way to an assembly prohibited by an order made under section 14A and direct that person not to proceed in the direction of the assembly. This power is only exercisable within the area covered by the order. Failure to comply with the police officer's direction is an offence.

An important qualification was made to the scope of these provisions in *DPP v Jones* (1999). The defendants were arrested while participating in a peaceful, unobstructive assembly at a roadside near Stonehenge. At the material time, an order made under section 14A prohibiting trespassory assemblies in the vicinity of Stonehenge was in force. The defendants were convicted of offences under section 14B. By a majority, the House of Lords quashed the convictions. Lord Irvine of Lairg L.C. held that the highway was a public place that the public might enjoy for any reasonable purpose, provided that the activity in question did not amount to a public or private nuisance and did not obstruct the highway by unreasonably impeding the public's primary right to pass and re-pass. Even in advance of the entry into force of the Human Rights Act, the majority were prepared to find that within the qualifications stated there was a public right of peaceful assembly on the highway, a right not to be whittled down in the absence of clear statutory words.

Many assemblies, of course, will not be subject to the rules considered above because they are held indoors. Rallies and meetings are regulated in the first instance by the owner of the property in which they are held, which is often a local authority. Local authorities have statutory duties to make public buildings available for political meetings at election times (sections 95 and 96, Representation of the People Act 1983). Beyond that, the discretion enjoyed by local authorities over the management of their property, though wide, is not absolute (*Wheeler v Leicester CC* (1985); *R v Somerset CC, ex parte Fewings* (1995)). Moreover, local authorities cannot enter into contracts for the hire of a public building for a meeting and then withdraw without payment of damages for breach of contract when it is brought to the authority's attention that the meeting is being held by an unsavoury group: *Verrall v Great Yarmouth B.C.* (1981).

For completeness, note also that other, non-statutory controls on assemblies are possible. Interdict may lie to restrain an actual or anticipated demonstration (*McIntyre v Sheridan* (1993)). Those taking part in an assembly may also expose themselves to criminal sanctions (see next section) or civil liability. The possibility of being convicted of a criminal offence or being faced with liability in damages may well deter people from taking part in legitimate acts of assembly and protest.

PUBLIC ORDER OFFENCES

A substantial number of statutory offences exist in order to control various species of public disorder. Some are highly context-specific, such as the offence contained in section 97 of the Representation of the People Act 1983 (disturbing an election meeting) and the offence of "watching and besetting" as defined in section 241 of the Trade Union and Labour Relations (Consolidation) Act 1992, which is mostly employed in the context of industrial action. Others are more general in scope, including:

- The offence under section 1 of the Public Order Act 1936, which prohibits the wearing of uniforms signifying association with any political organisation or for the promotion of any political object in a public place or at a public meeting (*O'Moran v DPP* (1975)).
- Incitement to racial hatred contrary to section 17 of the Public Order Act 1986.
- Racially aggravated harassment contrary to section 50A of the Criminal Law (Consolidation) (Scotland) Act 1995, as inserted by section 33 of the Crime and Disorder Act 1998.
- Aggravated trespass contrary to section 68 of the Criminal Justice and Public Order Act 1994. The offence consists of trespassing on land in the open air with the intention of intimidating persons who are engaging in or about to engage in any lawful activity on that land or adjoining land, so as to deter them from doing so; or with the intention of otherwise obstructing or disrupting that activity.
- Obstruction of the highway contrary to section 53 of the Civic Government (Scotland) Act 1982, which provides that any person who "being on foot in a public place—(a) obstructs, along with another or others, the lawful passage of any other person and fails to desist on being required to do so by a constable in uniform; or (b) wilfully obstructs the lawful passage of any other person" is guilty of an offence. "Obstruct" does not mean to block the street completely.
- Obstructing a police officer in the execution of his duty contrary to section 41 of the Police (Scotland) Act 1967. This provides that any person who "assaults, resists, obstructs, molests or hinders a constable in the execution of his duty ... shall be guilty of an offence". At least in the past, it had to be shown that "the obstruction had some physical aspect" (*per* Lord Fleming, *Curlett v McKechnie* (1938)). However, more recent cases suggest an attentuation of the physical element of the offence. In *Skeen v Shaw* (1979) it was suggested that "hinders" may not require more than a minimal physical element, even if "assaults" or "obstructs" clearly do.
- Mobbing and rioting, a common law offence constituted by participation in an illegal mob having a common criminal purpose: *Hancock v H.M. Advocate* (1981).

BREACH OF THE PEACE

The nature of the offence

The police are enjoined by section 17, Police (Scotland) Act 1967 to prevent disorder, and are empowered at common law to prevent or restrain breaches of the peace actual or anticipated. This, coupled with the significant breadth of the offence, confers on the police a wide and flexible power for maintaining public order.

In *Raffaelli v Heatley* (1949) the Lord Justice-Clerk held that:

"[W]here something is done in breach of public order or decorum which might reasonably be expected to lead to the lieges being alarmed or upset or tempted to make reprisals at their own hand, the circumstances are such as to amount to a breach of the peace."

The offence is not confined to disorderly or aggressive conduct. On the contrary, it was held in *Montgomery v McLeod* (1977) that:

"There is no limit to the kind of conduct which may give rise to a charge of breach of the peace. All that is required is that there must be some conduct such as to excite the reasonable apprehension to which we have drawn attention [*i.e.* that mischief may ensue] or such as to create alarm and disturbance to the lieges in fact."

But nobody need actually be alarmed or disturbed by the conduct in question, nor need there be an actual danger of mischief ensuing in the form of reprisal in response to the conduct complained of. Lord Dunpark stated clearly in *Wilson v Brown* (1982) (a case involving high-spirited football fans) that "[p]ositive evidence of actual harm, upset, annoyance or disturbance created by reprisal is not a prerequisite of conviction."

Thus alarm or disturbance may be treated as a matter of reasonable inference from the circumstances. Put shortly, then, conduct of a relatively inoffensive kind, which as a matter of fact upset or alarmed nobody, may suffice to constitute a breach of the peace, and it is on this basis that the power of the police to infringe upon freedom of expression and assembly is premised.

Since the entry into force of the Human Rights Act, however, it has been necessary to show that any restriction imposed upon the Convention rights is "prescribed by law" in the sense that the restriction is accessible to those it concerns and is formulated with sufficient precision to enable them to foresee with reasonable certainty the consequences that their actions may entail. In *McLeod v United Kingdom* (1999) and *Steel v United Kingdom* (1999), the European Court of Human Rights accepted that the concept of breach of the peace in English law satisfied this requirement in so far as "it is now sufficiently established that a breach of the peace is committed only when an individual causes harm to persons or property, or acts in a manner the natural consequences of which would be to provoke violence in others". This is plainly narrower that the concept of breach of the peace in Scots law, as Lord Coulsfield conceded in *Smith v Donnelly* (2001). There, the appellant was convicted of breach of the peace after taking part in a demonstration outside a naval base. She argued that her prosecution contravened the prohibition in Article 7 of the Convention on retrospective criminal penalties, on the basis that breach of the peace as understood in Scots law failed to define with sufficient clarity the forms of behaviour it proscribed. Lord Coulsfield agreed that in some of the authorities, a breach of the peace had been held established on "grounds which might charitably be described as tenuous". Having reviewed the leading cases, however, the Appeal Court held that the core meaning of the offence, at least, was sufficiently clear to meet the requirements of Article 7 (with which the European Court of Human

Rights agreed in *Lucas v United Kingdom* (2003), a decision on admissibility). Subsequently, in *Jones v Carnegie* (2004), a Court of Five Judges reviewed the law of Scotland in relation to breach of the peace in the context of Articles 10 and 11 of the ECHR, and again was satisfied that the prosecution and conviction of the appellants (with one exception) did not involve an unjustifiable interference with their Convention rights.

Where the police reasonably anticipate a breach of the peace occurring, they may—indeed, must—intervene to avert it. This might involve uninvited entry into private premises, the imposition of conditions on public meetings over and above any imposed pursuant to statutory powers, or the dispersal or even outright prevention of public assemblies. Notwithstanding the recent case law which finds the concept of breach of the peace to be essentially compatible with the ECHR (at least for the purposes of the "prescribed by law" requirement), it will still require to be shown in particular cases that action taken for the legitimate aim of preserving public order and preventing breaches of the peace was proportionate to the threat perceived.

Power to enter private premises

In *Thomas v Sawkins* (1935) police officers attended a meeting, anticipating that breaches of the peace might occur. The organiser of the meeting, Mr Thomas, asked the police officers to leave, and when they refused made as if to remove an officer by force. Another officer, P.C. Sawkins, physically restrained Mr Thomas, who then prosecuted P.C. Sawkins for assault. The court held that the police had been lawfully on the premises and that therefore P.C. Sawkins had not assaulted Mr Thomas. Avory J. held that "the police officers in question had reasonable grounds for believing that, if they were not present, ... a breach of the peace would take place. To prevent ... a breach of the peace, the police were entitled to enter and remain on the premises."

More broadly, Lord Hewart C.J. held that "[I]t is part of the preventative power, and, therefore, part of the preventative duty of the police, in cases where there are ... reasonable grounds of apprehension [of a breach of the peace] to enter and remain on private premises."

In other words, neither express statutory authority nor a warrant is necessary for the police to enter private premises uninvited where a breach of the peace is occurring or is reasonably anticipated. For England and Wales, this common law power was preserved by section 17(6) of the Police and Criminal Evidence Act 1984, the exercise of which was considered by the European Court of Human Rights in *McLeod v United Kingdom* (1999). There it was held that the applicant's right to respect for her private life and home under Article 8 of the Convention was infringed by two police officers who entered her home and who failed to prevent the entry of her ex-husband when he arrived uninvited to recover property said (by him) to be his. The European Court did not find the power under section 17(6) was *per se* incompatible with Article 8, but found that the manner of its exercise in the circumstances of this case—the applicant, who might have objected to her ex-husband's behaviour, was not even in the house at the material time—was disproportionate to the aim of preventing disorder. It would therefore seem that, in order to avoid censure under the Human Rights Act, the police will need to be able to point to a reasonably imminent threat to public order before entering private premises.

Power to impose conditions on public meetings
In the Irish case of *Humphries v Connor* (1864), a police officer requested Mrs Humphries to remove an orange lily from her jacket to prevent a breach of the peace amongst an antagonistic crowd. When she refused, he removed it himself. Mrs Humphries brought an action for assault, but the court, by a majority, accepted the need to prevent a breach of the peace as a good defence.

A step further was taken in *Duncan v Jones* (1936). Mrs Duncan was preparing to address a crowd outside an unemployment training centre. She had spoken at the same place 14 months before and a disturbance had ensued. To avert the risk of further disturbance, a police officer asked her to move away from the training centre and deliver her speech in a nearby street. She refused, and was charged with and convicted of obstructing a police officer in the execution of his duty. The court observed that once the police officer had formed a reasonable apprehension of a breach of the peace, "it then became his duty to prevent anything which in his view would cause that breach of the peace. While he was taking steps so to do, he was wilfully obstructed by [Mrs Duncan]."

Thirdly, in *Piddington v Bates* (1961), a police officer attending a trade dispute at a factory took the view that two pickets at each entrance were sufficient, and gave instructions accordingly in order to preserve the peace. Mr Piddington attempted to defy these instructions. He was convicted of obstructing a police officer in the execution of his duty.

These cases illustrate that the police have the power at common law to impose time, place and manner conditions on assemblies independently of their statutory powers under section 14 of the Public Order Act 1986. Nor are these common law powers subject to the limitations contained in section 14. They would apply to assemblies of less than 20 persons, indoors or outdoors. Similarly, a reasonable apprehension of a breach of the peace would seem to involve something less than a risk of "serious public disorder, serious damage to property or serious disruption of the life of the community". It does not follow from this that the actions of the police in these cases would now fall to be impugned as contrary to the ECHR. Nevertheless there is now a more rigorous burden upon the authorities to justify their actions as a proportionate response to a threat of disorder.

Power to disperse assemblies

The power to order an assembly to disperse, if necessary to prevent a breach of the peace, is but an aspect of the power to impose conditions. Note, however, that a lawful and peaceable assembly as much as a noisy and disorderly one may be ordered to disperse if it is attracting a "hostile audience": it is within the discretion of police officers at the scene to break up the assembly rather than deal with hecklers. Thus in *Deakin v Milne* (1882), Salvation Army marches in Arbroath had attracted the aggressive opposition, as Salvation Army marches throughout Britain were apt to do at the time, of the so-called Skeleton Army. To preserve the peace, Arbroath magistrates banned Salvation Army marches. The Salvationists defied the ban and were convicted of breaching the ban and breach of the peace. The validity of the ban and the convictions were affirmed by the High Court. The Lord Justice-Clerk held that "the assembling of persons, and the behaviour of persons when they so assemble, shall be within the law. But when it leads to a breach of the peace, however good the intentions of the persons may be, the magistrates are entitled to interfere".

Beatty v Gilbanks (1882) was an English case having similar facts, but which was differently decided. Field J. considered that the Salvation Army marches caused no disturbance of the peace:

> "[O]n the contrary … the disturbance that did take place was caused entirely by the unlawful and unjustifiable interference of the Skeleton Army … and … but for the opposition and molestation offered to the Salvationists by these other persons, no disturbance of any kind would have taken place."

Powerful as *Beatty v Gilbanks* is as an expression of civil liberty, its authority was diminished by the later cases of *Duncan v Jones* and *Piddington v Bates*. It has been held by the European Court of Human Rights, however, that freedom of assembly is a positive as well as negative right. In other words, it entitles one not merely to be left alone in the enjoyment of one's right, but also to the support and protection of public authorities where others would seek to prevent one exercising one's freedom. Hecklers have no veto in the jurisprudence of the European Court. The first duty of the police when faced with a situation such as that in *Beatty v Gilbanks* must therefore be to separate the opposing sides or to move a counter-demonstration on. Simply to order all persons to disperse would seem disproportionate, unless the threat of disorder is imminent and grave.

Power to prevent assemblies

During the miners' strike of 1984 to 1985, the police power to prevent breaches of the peace was used to stop assemblies forming altogether. In Scotland, the police turned back vehicles carrying miners to prevent them forming mass pickets at Hunterston ore terminal and Ravenscraig steelworks. In England, police road blocks were set up to prevent miners leaving their own counties (such as the Dartford Tunnel roadblock stopping miners from Kent travelling to picket lines on the Nottinghamshire coalfield) and to keep them away from the vicinity of collieries. Attempts to defy police directions were met with arrest and charge, usually for obstructing a police officer in the execution of his duty. A report on the policing of the miners' strike likened these practices to "the Soviet internal passport system or South African pass laws", but their legality was confirmed in *Moss v McLachlan* (1985). Four striking miners appealed against their convictions for obstructing a police officer on the basis that he was not acting in the execution of his duty because he had no power to turn them back or to refuse to let them proceed. Skinner J. held:

> "Provided [the senior police officers] present honestly and reasonably form the opinion that there is a real risk of a breach of the peace in the sense that it is close proximity both in place and time, then the conditions exist for reasonable preventive acting including, if necessary, the measures taken in this case."

The principle established in *Moss* was recently endorsed by the Court of Appeal in *R (Laporte) v Chief Constable of Gloucestershire Constabulary* (2005). The applicant was a passenger on a coach travelling from London to take part in a demonstration at RAF Fairford against the war in Iraq. The coach was stopped by police officers some five kilometres by road from the air base, the police having received intelligence that hard-line activists, who had caused disorder at previous demonstrations at the base, were expected to attend. Various items, including tools and balaclava helmets, were found in the coach. None of the passengers took responsibility for them. The officer in charge of policing the demonstration thereupon gave instructions to a number of officers to escort the coach back to London, which was done. However, while the Court of Appeal accepted that the officer in charge had reasonably formed the view that breaches of the peace might occur if the protestors were permitted to continue to Fairford, it held that he had acted disproportionately in having the coach escorted back to London and not allowing it to stop: "the passengers were virtually prisoners in the coaches for the length of the journey."

12. JUDICIAL REVIEW

THE SCOPE OF JUDICIAL REVIEW

Judicial review invokes the supervisory jurisdiction of the Court of Session, as distinct from its appellate jurisdiction. It is concerned with the legality or validity of the acts and decisions of (primarily) governmental and other public bodies, not with the merits of those acts and decisions. In 1985, a special procedure was introduced to facilitate access to the supervisory jurisdiction (see Chapter 58 of the Rules of the Court of Session). The leading modern authority on the scope of the supervisory jurisdiction, and hence of judicial review, is *West v Secretary of State for Scotland* (1992), where Lord President Hope held that:

"The Court of Session has power, in the exercise of its supervisory jurisdiction, to regulate the process by which decisions are taken by any person or body to whom a jurisdiction, power or authority has been delegated or entrusted by statute, agreement or any other instrument ... The cases in which the exercise of the supervisory jurisdiction is appropriate involve a tripartite relationship between the person or body to whom the jurisdiction, power or authority has been delegated or entrusted, the person or body by whom it has been delegated or entrusted and the person or persons in respect of or for whose benefit that jurisdiction, power or authority is to be exercised."

This makes clear that review is not confined to the statutory powers of administrative bodies. Prerogative powers are also, in principle, reviewable: *CCSU v Minister for the Civil Service* (1985). Equally, the supervisory jurisdiction may also extend to the acts and decisions of bodies which are not obviously "public", provided a reviewable jurisdiction exists (*e.g. Forbes v Underwood* (1886); *St Johnstone FC v Scottish Football Association* (1965); *Bank of Scotland v Investment Management Regulatory Organisation* (1989)).

Note also that just because a body is "public" does not mean that all of its acts and decisions will be subject to review. In *West* itself, it was held that the dispute between Mr West and the Secretary of State was essentially contractual, relating to the terms and conditions of Mr West's employment as a prison officer. It therefore failed Lord Hope's "tripartite relationship" test. But in other cases of public employment, *e.g. Rooney v Chief Constable, Strathclyde Police* (1996) and *Maclean v Glasgow City Council* (1997), review was held to be competent even though the petitions involved questions of an individual's contract. It may be that, where the court finds difficulty in applying the "tripartite relationship" test to the facts before it, the test collapses into something akin to the public/private law divide adopted to determine the scope of review in England. Nevertheless, uncertainties at the edges should not blind you to the fact of certainty at the core.

TITLE AND INTEREST

A petitioner must show title and interest to sue. For an individual to have title, "he must be a party (using the word in its widest sense) to some legal relationship which gives him some right which the person against whom he raises the action either infringes or denies" (*D & J Nicol v Dundee Harbour Trustees* (1915), *per* Lord Dunedin). In that case, the pursuers were held to have title to sue as harbour ratepayers: "members of a constituency erected by Act of Parliament ... and ... persons for whose benefit the harbour is kept up". Thus, title may be derived from the statutory relationship created between the parties by Act of Parliament. In the absence of a direct statutory relationship, title to sue may be founded on a statutory function owed to the public as a whole or to a class of the public (*Wilson v IBA* (1979)). However, where a statutory function is drawn more narrowly or specifically, those falling outwith its ambit will be denied title to sue despite a demonstrable interest to do so (*e.g. Paisley Taxi Owners' Association v Renfrew District Council* (1988); *Glasgow Rape Crisis Centre v Home Secretary* (2000)).

The concept of interest was explained by Lord Ardwell in *Swanson v Manson* (1907) as follows:

> "The grounds for this rule are (1) that the law courts of the country are not instituted for the purpose of deciding academic questions of law, but for settling disputes where any of the lieges has a real interest to have a question determined which involves his pecuniary rights or his status; and (2) that no person is entitled to subject another to the trouble and expense of a litigation unless he has some real interest to enforce or protect."

Lord Clyde held in *Scottish Old People's Welfare Council, Petrs* (1987) that the phrase "pecuniary rights or status" should not be regarded as "an exhaustive or complete description of what may comprise an interest". Nevertheless, in that case, his Lordship held that the petitioners' interest was insufficient to give them a right to sue. The petitioners, a pressure group campaigning on behalf of the elderly, challenged the legality of instructions in a government circular concerning the allocation of cold weather payments to social security claimants. They lacked sufficient interest because they were "not suing as a body of potential claimants but as a body working to protect and advance the interests of the aged".

It is in the public interest that all official decisions should be made lawfully; it is also in the public interest that public bodies should not be exposed to vexatious litigation by busybodies. But the approach taken to sufficiency of interest in Scotland does not countenance an active role in the supervision of administrative legality for pressure groups and genuinely concerned, if not directly interested, members of the public (notwithstanding occasional hints to the contrary, *e.g. Cockenzie and Port Seton Community Council v East Lothian DC* (1996), *Educational Institute for Scotland v Robert Gordon University* (1996)). It should however be noted that since 2000, it has been possible for a person not directly affected by an issue raised in a petition for judicial review to apply to the court for leave to intervene in the petition. In any case, pressure groups have always been free to fund, if not front, "public interest" litigation.

THE GROUNDS FOR JUDICIAL REVIEW

In *CCSU v Minister for the Civil Service* (1985), Lord Diplock summarised the grounds on which judicial review may be sought:

> "Judicial review has I think developed to a stage today when one can conveniently classify under three heads the grounds on which administrative action is subject to control by judicial review. The first ground I would call 'illegality', the second 'irrationality' and the third 'procedural impropriety'."

These three headings—illegality, irrationality and procedural impropriety—are compendious. Each has therefore to be broken down into smaller segments if you are to understand the various grounds on which an administrative act or decision may be challenged. You must also remember that the principles discussed below do not lend themselves to simplistic or rigid analysis: they interact, overlap and are open to future adaptation and extension. Lord Diplock himself referred to the possible future development of review on the basis of proportionality, which, as we shall see, has now been accepted (in appropriate cases) as an independent ground of review.

ILLEGALITY

In the most straightforward sense, an act will be illegal or *ultra vires* if it is done without legal authority. Thus, in *McColl v Strathclyde RC* (1983), the council was held to have acted *ultra vires* in adding fluoride to the public water supply. The duty laid on the council by the Water (Scotland) Act 1980 was to supply wholesome water. The fluoride was added not to improve the wholesomeness of the water but to improve dental health.

Error of law

A related situation is where the decision-maker misconstrues the provisions which empower him to act or decide. As Lord President Emslie put it in *Wordie Property Co v Secretary of State for Scotland* (1984), a decision may be invalid if it is based on a "material error of law going to the root of the question for determination". As this implies, not every error of law will suffice to invalidate a decision. In the first place, a given error may not be sufficiently "material" to engage the supervisory jurisdiction. It is also clear that, whatever may be the position in England, Scots law continues to recognise a distinction between reviewable errors of law and "non-jurisdictional" errors that the decision-maker is free to make subject to any right of appeal (see *Watt v Lord Advocate* (1979) and *Codona v Appeal Tribunal of the Showmen's Guild of Great Britain* (2002)).

Where the exercise of statutory powers is concerned, review for error of law might be taken to mean that the decision maker must understand every condition of the exercise of his power correctly, with the courts being the ultimate arbiter of correctness. However, in practice, the conditions for the exercise of a statutory power are often cast in terms which are not self-executing but which call for the exercise of judgment and discretion. In *R v Monopolies and Mergers Commission, ex parte South Yorkshire Transport* (1993), for example, the Commission had the power to act if it formed the view that a monopoly situation existed in a "substantial part" of the United Kingdom. The Commission exercised this power in respect of the provision of bus services in an area of the north of England amounting to 1.65 per cent of the total area of the United Kingdom. South Yorkshire Transport argued that the Commission had acted on a misconstruction of the conditions for the exercise of its power, contending that 1.65 per cent could not be regarded as a "substantial part" of the United Kingdom. The House of Lords disagreed, warning against "the dangers of taking an inherently imprecise term and, by redefining it, thrusting on it a spurious degree of precision. The question is whether the Commission placed the phrase broadly in the right part of the spectrum of possible meanings [and] within the permissible field of judgment."

Even so, in appropriate cases—particularly those involving fundamental rights—the courts are prepared to narrow the "spectrum of possible meanings" to such an extent that, effectively, there is only one right answer to a given question of statutory interpretation, and a decision will be struck down for error of law if the decision maker has failed to answer that question correctly (*R v Home Secretary, ex parte Adan and Aitseguer* (2000)).

Error of fact

Where the exercise of decision-making power depends upon the "precedent establishment of an objective fact", alleged errors of fact are reviewable (*R v Home Secretary, ex parte Khawaja* (1984); *Tan Te Lam v Superintendent of the Tai A Chau Detention Cente* (1997)). Beyond that, however, the position was generally taken, at least until recently, to be as stated by Lord Brightman in *R v Hillingdon London Borough Council, ex parte Puhlhofer* (1986): "it is the duty of the court to leave the decision [as to the existence of a fact] to the public body to whom Parliament has entrusted the decision making power, save in a case where it is obvious that the public body, consciously or unconsciously, is acting perversely". This captures the natural deferential reflex of a court of general but limited jurisdiction to the findings of fact made by a decision maker, who is often a highly experienced expert in his field, who may well have had the advantages of seeing and hearing witnesses and testing their evidence, and whose authority is not lightly to be usurped by the court. It does not, however, address the situation where, although not acting perversely or unreasonably in the *Wednesbury* sense, the decision maker nonetheless arrives at a decision on an incorrect factual basis, perhaps because not all the relevant evidence was laid before him or because the significance of the available evidence was misunderstood.

In *Secretary of State for Education v Tameside Metropolitan Borough Council* (1977) Scarman L.J. in the Court of Appeal referred to "misunderstanding or ignorance of an established and relevant fact" as a matter capable of attracting judicial intervention in the context of review. Academic commentators interpreted *Tameside* as establishing mere factual mistake as a ground for judicial review, although it was not until *R v Criminal Injuries Compensation Board, ex parte A* (1999) that the House of Lords recognised mistake of fact as providing an independent head of review. Having surveyed the case law, the Court of Appeal held in *E v Secretary of State for the Home Department* (2004) that the reviewability of factual errors rested on the principle of fairness. Specifically, unfairness arose where the following conditions were met:

"First, there must have been a mistake as to an existing fact, including a mistake as to the availability of evidence on a particular matter. Secondly, the fact or evidence must have been 'established', in the sense that it was uncontentious and objectively verifiable. Thirdly, the appellant (or his advisers) must not have been responsible for the mistake. Fourthly, the mistake must have played a material (not necessarily decisive) part in the tribunal's reasoning."

The greater preparedness of the court to intervene to correct errors of fact may in part have been prompted by the entry into force of the Human Rights Act. This is principally because judicial review might otherwise fail to satisfy Article 6 of the ECHR, so far as it requires a right of recourse against a decision to a higher court or tribunal having "full jurisdiction". Thus in *R (Javed) v Home Secretary* (2001), it was held that, although historically reluctant to evaluate evidence when reviewing decisions of the executive, the courts now have a positive duty to give effect to the ECHR and to ensure that there is an effective remedy in cases of suspected breaches of Convention rights. Therefore, where an executive decision needs to be reviewed on the facts, the court is competent to carry out that exercise once the relevant material is placed before it. In this case, the court quashed the Home Secretary's decision to include and retain Pakistan in the list of designated countries as a country in which it appeared to him that there was in general no serious risk of persecution, on the basis that such a conclusion was simply not justified by Pakistan's human rights record. The applicants were thereupon able successfully to challenge the decision to reject their applications for asylum.

The constitutional justification for review on jurisdictional grounds is compelling, especially in relation to the review of statutory powers. Parliament confers powers which are limited in terms of the statutory wording. It is not for the donee of such powers to enlarge the scope of the authority that Parliament intended him to have by using his power as the basis for action which was not in fact authorised; or, having misinterpreted the wording of the statute, by using his power on an erroneous basis of law or fact. The role of the courts is to police the boundaries of powers so conferred, in order to ensure that, in accordance with Parliament's intention, the donee remains within the ambit of his authority. But review under the heading of illegality does not end here, and as we move further out, this constitutional justification for review may become somewhat attenuated. Here we are concerned with illegality as *irrelevancy* or *impropriety of purpose* or *bad faith*.

Irrelevant considerations

First, the courts see it as implicit in any grant of power that it must be exercised having regard to all relevant considerations and excluding any irrelevant ones. A number of cases involving decisions taken partly in furtherance of political or moral beliefs illustrate the point. In *Gerry Cottle's Circus v City of Edinburgh D.C.* (1990), the council refused a licence to the circus on the basis of its policy against circuses featuring performing animals. The refusal was held unlawful in that the council had failed to have regard to its statutory duties and powers, and in that this decision was inconsistent with other decisions it had made in the same area. In *Bromley LBC v Greater London Council* (1983), the House of Lords held that the Greater London Council had acted illegally in implementing a manifesto pledge of the majority Labour group to reduce fares on public transport in London. This was because the Greater London Council could not use its powers to achieve a social policy which conflicted with statutory obligations to run London transport according to ordinary business principles; and because the fare reduction involved a breach of the council's fiduciary duty to ratepayers (see to like effect, *e.g. Roberts v Hopwood* (1926); *R v Somerset County Council, ex parte Fewings* (1995)).

Improper purposes

The use of powers to further improper purposes is closely related to the failure to take account of relevant considerations, or the taking into account of irrelevant ones, as a form of illegality. In *Padfield v Minister of Agriculture* (1968), the House of Lords held that discretion was entrusted to the minister so that he might promote the policy and purposes of the legislation, and that he was not at liberty to thwart those purposes by misinterpreting them. A Scottish case on this point is *Highland RC v British Railways Board* (1996). The Railways Act 1993 laid down procedures to be followed if it is proposed to close a line or withdraw services. Having resolved to withdraw the Fort William-London sleeper service, and in an attempt to avoid observance of the closure procedures, British Rail ran "ghost trains" on the line, so that there was, arguably, a "railway passenger service" being provided but one which was not being used. The First Division held this device to be illegal as tending to frustrate the policy and purposes envisaged by Parliament in the legislation.

Bad faith

It is difficult to conceive of decisions which are flawed for bad faith but which could not be attacked on grounds of irrelevancy or impropriety of purpose. The courts may, however, choose to couch their judgments in terms of bad faith where dishonesty, malice or spite is present. Thus in *Roncarelli v Duplessis* (1959), Mr Roncarelli's liquor licence was revoked on the direction of the Premier of Québec. The direction was motivated by Mr Roncarelli's repeated provision of bail for fellow Jehovah's Witnesses, who had been charged with offences relating to the distribution of religious literature. Unsurprisingly, the revocation of the licence was struck down.

Improper delegation

As a rule, a person who exercises a power vested in another will act without legal authority. But this rule is not absolute. Delegation is permissible in certain circumstances, having regard to such factors as the statutory background, the nature of the power which is delegated and the type of person or body to which it is delegated.

Thus it is accepted that where powers are granted to a minister, they can validly be exercised by officials in the minister's department (*Carltona v Commissioner for Works* (1943)) unless the enabling statute makes clear that the power must be exercised by the minister personally (*Lavender & Son v Minister for Housing and Local Government* (1970)). In *R v Home Secretary, ex parte Oladehinde* (1991), the House of Lords held that the Secretary of State could lawfully delegate his power to deport to immigration officers of sufficient grade and experience, provided that this involved no conflict with the officers' own statutory duties. In general, then, it must be shown that delegation was, expressly or impliedly, within the contemplation of the legislation.

Unlawful fettering of discretion

It is implicit in every grant of discretionary power that the donee of the power remains free to exercise that discretion whenever necessary. He may not bind himself in advance as to the way his discretion might be exercised. Thus, public authorities may not enter into contracts binding them to act in a certain way (*Ayr Harbour Trustees v Oswald* (1883)). Only if the contract is compatible with the authority's statutory duties and powers will it be valid (*R v Hammersmith and Fulham LBC, ex parte Beddowes* (1987)). Similarly, assurances given or representations made by a public authority do not bind it, if the assurance or representation was beyond the powers of the public authority in the first place or if the public interest (in allowing the authority the free play of its discretion) outweighs any unfairness to an individual who has relied on the assurance or representation: for discussion of this issue (see *R v East Sussex County Council, ex parte Reprotech (Pebsham) Ltd* (2003)).

It is not only by contract or representation that a public body may unlawfully fetter its discretion. Where a public authority has to make many individual decisions in the same area, consistency of decision-making and administrative efficiency may well demand the adoption of general policies to guide the decision-making process. This is acceptable so long as the policy does not amount to a blanket rule. Policies applied in an over-rigid manner which fails to allow for individuated decisions where necessary will be illegal (*British Oxygen Co v Board of Trade* (1971); *R v Home Secretary, ex parte Venables and Thompson* (1998)).

Note, however, that assurances, representations or policies may generate legitimate expectations which will be protected by the courts. This is discussed below.

IRRATIONALITY AND PROPORTIONALITY

Even though judicial review is concerned with the legal validity of a given decision, as distinct from its "correctness", this is not to say that the court on review has no control over the substance of a decision. A decision which was "unreasonable" (or "irrational", as Lord Diplock preferred to express it in *CCSU*) could be struck down by a court on review. However, the threshold of unreasonableness necessary to attract judicial intervention was (and in certain circumstances, still is) pitched very high for, as Lord Greene M.R. explained in *Associated Provincial Picture Houses v Wednesbury Corporation* (1948):

> "It is not what the court considers unreasonable ... If it is what the court considers unreasonable, the court may very well have different views to that of the local authority on matters of high public policy of this kind ... The effect of the legislation is not to set the court up as an arbiter of the correctness of one view over another. It is the local authority that are set in that position and, provided they act ... within the four corners of their jurisdiction, this court, in my opinion, cannot interfere."

This expresses the courts' sensitivity to their constitutional position in the context of review. Even review on the grounds of relevancy and propriety of purpose, although it is presented as a technical matter of statutory interpretation, may risk trespassing on the merits of discretionary decisions. In the context of review for irrationality, this danger is inescapably apparent. In terms of the *Wednesbury* doctrine, therefore, a decision could only be struck down for unreasonableness where it was "unreasonable in the sense that the court considers it to be a decision that no reasonable body could have come to" (*per* Lord Greene M.R., *Wednesbury*) or "so outrageous in its defiance of logic or of accepted moral standards that no sensible person who had applied his mind to the question to be decided could have arrived at it" (*per* Lord Diplock, *CCSU*). But while such judicial deference may be appropriate in some contexts, it is not appropriate across the board. The courts' response to criticism of the poverty of the *Wednesbury* principle was to insist upon more compelling justification for administrative decisions affecting fundamental rights, even in advance of the entry into force of the Human Rights Act 1998 (see *e.g. Bugdaycay v Home Secretary* (1987); *R v Ministry of Defence, ex parte Smith* (1996); *Abdadou v Home Secretary* (1998)). As Lord Bingham MR put it in *Smith*:

> "The court may not interfere with an administrative decision on substantive grounds save where the court is satisfied that the decision is unreasonable in the sense that it is beyond the range of responses open to a reasonable decision maker. But in judging whether the decision maker has exceeded this margin of appreciation, the human rights context is important. The more substantial the interference with human rights, the more the court will require by way of justification before it is satisfied that the decisions are reasonable in the sense outlined above."

Thus adjusted, review for unreasonableness begins to resemble the principle of proportionality, a feature of the jurisprudence of both the European Court of Justice and the European Court of Human Rights. Proportionality involves a more rigorous examination of the relationship between administrative ends and means, and it must now be applied by the courts where reliance is placed upon one or more of the Convention rights. As Lord Steyn observed in *R (Daly) v Home Secretary* (2001), even the heightened scrutiny test developed in *Bugdaycay* and *Smith* may not be sufficient for the protection of human rights: proportionality, unlike *Wednesbury*, may require the reviewing court to assess the balance struck by the decision-maker, not merely whether it is within a range of rational or reasonable responses; and may require attention to be directed to the relative weights accorded by the decision-maker to specific rights and considerations.

Two points should be noted. First, "the greater intensity of judicial review which is required by the proportionality test does not arise in domestic law where there is no engagement of a Convention right and no fundamental right is in play. The test remains *Wednesbury*" (*R (Medway*

Council) v Secretary of State for Transport (2002), *per* Maurice Kay L.J.; see also *R (Association of British Civilian Internees—Far Eastern Region) v Secretary of State for Defence* (2003)). This position may change, but for the present the converse of proportionality review is adherence to traditional *Wednesbury* standards in areas not touching upon Community law or fundamental rights, where considerations of relative expertise and institutional competence and/or considerations of democratic accountability for decisions call for continued deference to the judgment of the primary decision-maker. Secondly, however, it should not be assumed that judicial deference has no place in the context of proportionality review. Even here, the courts require to accord a degree of latitude to the primary decision-maker for the reasons explained by Lord Hope in *R v Director of Public Prosecutions, ex parte Kebilene* (2000):

> "Difficult choices may have to be made by the executive or the legislature between the rights of the individual and the needs of society. In some circumstances it will be appropriate for the courts to recognise that there is an area of judgment within which the judiciary will defer, on democratic grounds, to the considered opinion of the elected body or person whose act or decision is said to be incompatible with the Convention ... It will be easier for such an area of judgment to be recognised where the Convention itself requires a balance to be struck, much less so where the right is stated in terms which are unqualified. It will be easier for it to be recognised where the issues involve questions of social or economic policy, much less so where the rights are of high constitutional importance or are of a kind where the courts are especially well placed to assess the need for protection."

PROCEDURAL IMPROPRIETY

In the narrow sense, this head of review may involve no more than failure to comply with prescribed procedural requirements. More broadly, the courts regard it as implicit in every grant of power that the power will be exercised in accordance with the rules of natural justice: the rule against bias (*nemo iudex in sua causa*) and the right to a fair hearing (*audi alteram partem*). From these twin principles, the courts have developed a general duty to act fairly, the content of which varies according to context and circumstances. Increasingly, fairness is held to require that reasons are given for decisions. Similarly, fairness may involve protection of legitimate expectations.

Compliance with procedural requirements

Legislation often prescribes specific procedural requirements which the decision-maker should observe in the process of reaching a decision, such as the giving of notice to third parties, or a requirement of prior consultation. A distinction is often drawn here between mandatory and directory procedural requirements. Broadly speaking, compliance with the former is necessary for the validity of a decision; compliance with the latter is not. Note, however, that the distinction has not met with universal approval. In *London and Clydeside Estates v Aberdeen DC* (1980), Lord Hailsham LC regarded the distinction as over-rigid: the problem was one of degree rather than one of category. Failure to comply with a procedural requirement might amount to a fundamental flaw in the decision-making process. Equally, it might involve nothing more than a trivial defect which the courts would probably ignore. In most cases, the importance of a procedural requirement cannot be determined in the abstract, so that the better approach is to assess on a case by case basis how far a failure to comply has caused prejudice to the person concerned.

Natural justice: the rule against bias
It is well established that where a decision maker has a direct pecuniary or proprietary interest in the outcome of the decision making process, this operates as an automatic disqualification (*Dimes v Proprietors of the Grand Junction Canal* (1852)). The categories of automatic disqualification were extended by the decision of the House of Lords in *R v Bow Street Metropolitan Stipendiary Magistrate, ex parte Pinochet Ugarte (No. 2)* (2000), where it was held that:

> "[I]f, as in the present case, the matter at issue does not relate to money or economic advantage but is concerned with the promotion of the cause, the rationale disqualifying a judge applies just as much if the judge's decision will lead to the promotion of a cause in which the judge is involved together with one of the parties."

In such cases, then, disqualification is automatic and nothing more requires to be proved. If the decision maker proceeds to decide nevertheless, the decision cannot stand. However, the rule against bias also comes into play, even though the decision maker is not financially interested in the outcome and is not otherwise acting as a judge of his own cause, where in some other sense his conduct or behaviour may give rise to suspicion that he may not be impartial. For example, family or other personal connections may give rise to an inference of bias (*Metropolitan Property Co Ltd v Lannon* (1969)). So too may evidence of predisposition for or against a party on the part of the decision maker (*Bradford v McLeod* (1986); *R v Inner West London Coroner, ex parte Dallaglio* (1996)). In such circumstances, the test is whether a fair-minded observer, knowing the factors bearing on the allegation that the decision maker was biased, would consider that there was a real danger or real possibility that he might indeed have been biased (*Porter v Magill* (2002)). If a decision maker perceives a difficulty of this sort, he is bound to draw it to the attention of the parties. If they agree to his hearing the matter that is an end to it: the right to object is thereafter waived. If either or both objects to his sitting, however, he must recuse himself.

The authorities so far cited all concern challenges to judicial decisions, and in the past it appeared that a different test applied to decisions of administrative bodies. However, in *R v Environment Secretary, ex parte Kirkstall Valley Campaign Ltd* (1996), Sedley J. held that the administrative/judicial dichotomy is not determinative of the application of the rule against bias. Thus the *Pinochet* and *Porter* tests apply across the board. However, the dichotomy will continue to influence to rigour with which the rule applies:

> "[W]hat will differ from case to case is the significance of the interest and its degree of proximity or remoteness to the issue to be decided and whether, if it is not so insignificant or remote as to be discounted, the disqualified member has violated his disqualification by participating in the decision."

Natural justice: the right to a hearing and the duty to act fairly

Prior to the decision of the House of Lords in *Ridge v Baldwin* (1964), the courts tended to confine the application of the rules of natural justice to decisions of a judicial or quasi-judicial character. *Ridge* established (or revived) the broader application of natural justice. It was held in that case that a chief constable who was dismissable only for cause was entitled to notice of the charge against him and to an opportunity to be heard in his own defence before he could be lawfully dismissed.

The importance of *Ridge* lies in their Lordships' more general discussion of the principles of natural justice and their disapproval of the constraints imposed on their application by the judicial/administrative dichotomy. At the same time, however, the House of Lords gave little indication of where the right to a hearing should apply and to what extent. As court proceedings illustrate, the right involves, at its fullest, proceedings in public, notice of proceedings, the opportunity to make representations and lead evidence, cross-examination of witnesses, legal representation, reasons for the decision and the right to an appeal or re-hearing. If the principles of natural justice are to obtain in purely administrative situations, it is plain that the application of the right to a hearing, at least, must be qualified if the administrative process is not to be brought to a complete standstill.

In *Re H.K.* (1967), Lord Parker C.J. spoke not in terms of the principles of natural justice but of "fairness" and a "duty to act fairly". Even so, there remained a need for criteria to determine who should benefit from procedural protection and what, in particular situations, such protection should involve. To some extent, the old habits of classification lingered: "judicial" proceedings might still be expected to attract more in the way of procedural protection than "administrative" proceedings (see *Errington v Wilson* (1995)), and it was held in *Bates v Hailsham* (1972) that delegated legislative functions did not involve a need for a hearing at all.

Increasingly, however, the courts have focused on the nature of the right or interest (or legitimate expectation) alleged to be affected by the challenged decision. In *McInnes v Onslow-Fane* (1978), the Vice-Chancellor contrasted the positions of the holder of a licence whose licence is revoked; the individual who applies for renewal of a licence shortly to expire; and the initial applicant for a licence. In the first case, the individual is being deprived of a subsisting interest akin to a property right and as such "the right to an unbiased tribunal, the right to notice of the charges and the right to be heard in answer to the charges ... are plainly apt". In relation to the second category, it was held that "the legitimate expectation of a renewal of the licence ... is one which raises the question of what it is that has happened to make the applicant unsuitable for the ... licence for which he was previously thought suitable". Therefore, he is entitled to a higher degree of procedural protection than the initial applicant, from whom "nothing is being taken away, and in all normal circumstances there are no charges and so no requirement of an opportunity of being heard in answer to the charges".

In summary, there are three basic points to have in mind when considering the application of natural justice or fairness:

- The preliminary question of *entitlement* to procedural fairness is no longer affected by distinctions between the nature of the decision-making function and/or the nature of the rights or interest affected thereby.
- However, the *content* of the duty to act fairly is variable: "the so-called rules of natural justice are not engraved on tablets of stone ... What the requirements of fairness demand ... depends on the character of the decision-making body, the kind of decision it has to make, and the statutory or other framework in which it operates" (*per* Lord Bridge, *Lloyd v McMahon* (1987)).
- The nature of and impact upon the petitioner's rights or interests is not the only relevant factor in determining the content of the duty to act fairly. Certainly where statutory powers are concerned, the statutory background is important (although the courts will supplement a statutory procedural code to the extent necessary to secure fairness: *Lloyd v McMahon* (1987)). The overarching concern of the courts is to ensure that a fair hearing is provided, and they will willingly "supply the omission of the legislature" where it is deemed necessary to do so.

Fairness and legitimate expectations

The duty to act fairly applies not only where harm to an individual's legal rights or interests is in issue. In *Schmidt v Home Secretary* (1967), two American Scientology students had been admitted to the United Kingdom for a limited period. On the expiry of that period, the Home Secretary refused them an extension of leave to remain. The students challenged this decision on the grounds, *inter alia*, that it was made without a hearing. The Court of Appeal dismissed the action, but Lord Denning MR observed:

> "The speeches in *Ridge v Baldwin* show that an administrative body may, in a proper case, be bound to give a person who is affected by their decision an opportunity of making representations. It all depends on whether he has some right or interest or, I would add, some legitimate expectation, of which it would not be fair to deprive him without hearing what he has to say."

So, had the applicants' permits been revoked before they expired, they should have been able to make representations because they would have had a legitimate expectation of being allowed to stay in the United Kingdom for the permitted time. But they had neither a right nor a legitimate expectation of being allowed to stay for a longer period, and so an extension of time could be refused without reasons and without a hearing. The underlying principle here is that legitimate expectations induced by governmental conduct should not be thwarted by behaviour on the part of government which is unpredictable, irregular or arbitrary.

A legitimate expectation may be derived, in the first place, from an express promise or representation. In *Attorney General of Hong Kong v Ng Yuen Shiu* (1983), the Hong Kong authorities had announced that illegal immigrants would be interviewed, with each case being dealt with on its merits, before any decision was taken to expel them from the territory. The applicant had entered Hong Kong illegally some years previously and had in the meantime established a flourishing business. The authorities purported to expel him without an interview. The Privy Council held that, although the duty to act fairly might not generally apply to illegal immigrants, the Hong Kong authorities had by their assurances created a legitimate expectation of a hearing which should be enforced.

Secondly, a legitimate expectation may be derived from an implied representation based upon the past practice of the decision-maker. A representation, whether express or implied, must be "clear, unambiguous and devoid of relevant qualification" (*R v Inland Revenue Commissioners, ex parte MFK Underwriting Agencies* (1990)). Thus in *CCSU v Minister for the Civil Service* (1985), the established practice of consultation with staff unions at GCHQ before making changes in the terms and conditions of their service was held to generate a legitimate expectation of consultation (but see below). Similarly, in *R v Home Secretary, ex parte Khan* (1985), the Home Office issued a circular stating the criteria which the Home Secretary would apply in cases of international adoption. Relying on these criteria, the applicant sought entry clearance for his nephew from Pakistan. On the basis of different criteria, clearance was refused. Parker L.J. held that the Home Secretary could not depart from his stated policy "without affording interested persons a hearing and only then if the overriding public interest demands it".

This reference to the "public interest" serves to emphasise that the individual's legitimate expectation may be outweighed by competing considerations. *CCSU* again provides an example: the unions' legitimate expectation of consultation on the proposed ban on union membership was held to be overridden by the public interest in national security, which the minister claimed was compromised by industrial action at GCHQ. In general terms, it is obviously important that, notwithstanding the creation of legitimate expectations, public bodies should be able to alter their policies and practices as the public interest requires. But the doctrine of legitimate expectations serves to remind government that, in so doing, it must, in fairness, treat individuals' legitimate expectations with the degree of respect that is compatible with the wider public interest.

An issue only recently resolved is whether legitimate expectations attract only procedural, as distinct from substantive, protection. If the former, the courts can do no more than inquire whether the decision-maker acted fairly towards the applicant, in view of his legitimate expectation, before making his decision; if the latter, the courts may in appropriate cases examine the fairness of the outcome of the decision-making process to the holder of the expectation. In *R v North and East Devon Health Authority, ex parte Coughlan* (2000), the Court of Appeal confirmed that, in certain limited circumstances, a legitimate expectation of a substantive benefit could as a matter of fairness be enforced by the courts. The applicant, a severely disabled woman, had been promised a "home for life" in accommodation run by the health authority. The authority then decided to close the home and purported to move the applicant to other accommodation. The Court of Appeal held that, where a lawful promise or representation has induced a legitimate expectation of a substantive benefit, the court has the power to hold that to frustrate the expectation would be so unfair as to amount to an abuse of power. The authority for this proposition was derived from a series of cases in which the unfairness complained of was so marked as to amount to an excess or abuse of power (see *R v Inland Revenue Commissioners, ex parte Preston* (1985); *R v Inland Revenue Commissioners, ex parte Unilever plc* (1996); *R v National Lottery Commission, ex parte Camelot Group plc* (2000)).

Fairness and the duty to give reasons
It is still sometimes said that there is no general duty at common law to give reasons for decisions (*R v Higher Education Funding Council, ex parte Institute of Dental Surgery* (1994)). However, the exceptions that have been made to that general principle may suggest that the sum of the exceptions is now greater than the principle itself. For a general discussion, see the opinion of Lord Reed in *Tomkins v Lothian and Borders Police Board* (2005).

There are a number of rationales for requiring that reasons be provided. Reasons may be required where the effect of their absence is to frustrate a right of appeal or review. Alternatively, the courts might require reasons where necessary to rebut an inference of irrationality (*Padfield v Minister of Agriculture* (1968)). This was one of the grounds for the Court of Appeal decision in *R v Civil Service Appeal Board, ex parte Cunningham* (1991), where a prison officer who had been unfairly dismissed challenged the Board's decision to award him only £6,500 in circumstances where an industrial tribunal would have awarded two or three times as much. More broadly, however, the Court of Appeal also held that in the circumstances, reasons were required as a matter of fairness. The House of Lords followed this broader approach in *R v Home Secretary, ex parte Doody* (1994), which concerned the right of prisoners given mandatory life sentences to know the reasons for the determination of the "tariff" element of their sentences. Their Lordships held that the Home Secretary was under a duty to give reasons here both because fairness required it and because the absence of reasons, by making the detection of errors impossible, frustrated the prisoners' right to seek judicial review of the Home Secretary's decisions.

Where reasons are required, they must be "proper, adequate and intelligible". However, it is also well established that what are good reasons in any particular case depends very much on the circumstances of the case. Thus, in *Zia v Home Secretary* (1994), Lord Prosser reduced an immigration adjudicator's refusal of entry clearance on the grounds that the written reasons were unclear and insufficient. In *Safeway Stores v National Appeal Panel* (1996) it was held that the reasoning given in support of the Panel's decision was inadequate in that it merely paraphrased the applicable regulations without indicating what the real reasons and material considerations were.

APPENDIX: MODEL QUESTIONS AND ANSWERS

"The Diceyan account of the sovereignty of Parliament is no longer adequate to capture the 'top rule' of the British constitution." *Discuss.*

The term "top rule" was coined by legal philosopher HLA Hart. It is founded on the notion that any given legal order consists of a "hierarchy of norms". Each norm, or legal rule, derives its validity from a superior norm within the hierarchy. The top rule of the system is that to which, ultimately, the validity of all inferior norms may be traced. As the top rule of the system, it cannot derive its own validity from any other superior source. In that sense, its validity is a matter of political fact; it serves as the criterion of legal validity because it is accepted as such by constitutional actors, including (in particular) the courts.

Dicey identified the sovereignty of Parliament as the top rule of the British constitution, in the sense that Acts of Parliament are the highest form of law known to the constitution. Parliament may make or unmake any law whatever, and no person or body had the power to question the validity of or to set aside an Act of Parliament. The question asks you to comment on the adequacy of this account today, more than a century after it was formulated.

It is not necessary to test the Diceyan account by reference to each and every theoretical challenge it has faced. Given the wording of the question, it would suffice to note that, for much of the twentieth century, that account did indeed command general acceptance in the face of such challenges, not least from the courts (the only possible exceptions within these islands coming from the Scottish cases of *MacCormick v Lord Advocate* (1953) and *Gibson v Lord Advocate* (1975)). Towards the end of that century, however, real challenges were made to Diceyan orthodoxy and on a number of fronts.

The first major breach came with the acceptance, in the *Factortame* litigation (although presaged by earlier cases, such as *Macarthys Ltd v Smith* (1979)) that United Kingdom courts could pronounce on the compatibility of an Act of Parliament with directly effective provisions of Community law, and could grant interim relief by way of injunction or interdict to restrain the competent authority from applying such incompatible national legislation. This, the House of Lords held, was the inevitable consequence of Parliament's own choice as embodied in the European Communities Act 1972. This analysis finds an echo in the Human Rights Act 1998, section 4 of which confers on certain higher courts the power to make "declarations of incompatibility" in respect of provisions of Acts of Parliament which cannot be read and given effect in a manner compatible with the Convention rights. But two points should be noted. First, the courts cannot strike down provisions of an Act of Parliament for inconsistency with Community law or the Convention rights. Incompatibility does not denote invalidity. The courts can do no more than declare an incompatibility to exist; it is then for Parliament to take the necessary corrective action if it chooses to do so. To that extent, the legal truth of the Diceyan account may be said to survive. Secondly, in both cases, the jurisdiction of the courts to pronounce on the compatibility of Acts of Parliament with Community law and the Convention rights has its source in the enabling provisions of the 1972 Act and the 1998 Act respectively rather than in any assertion of competence by the courts themselves.

These developments have, however, compelled the courts to recognise one important qualification to Diceyan doctrine. For Dicey, it was implicit in the concept of the sovereignty of Parliament that the

Parliament for the time being was sovereign. Thus where two statutes conflicted, the later in time would prevail, having impliedly repealed the earlier measure to the extent of any inconsistency (as to this, see *Ellen Street Estates Limited v Minister of Health* (1934)). The decision in *Factortame* made plain that this doctrine of implied repeal did not apply to the European Communities Act 1972. Subsequently, in *Thoburn v Sunderland City Council* (2003), Laws L.J. held that this was also true of other "constitutional statutes", including the Union legislation of 1707, the Human Rights Act 1998 and the Scotland Act 1998. That is not to say that Parliament could not repeal such statutes. If Parliament wished to do so, however, it would require to do so expressly. Mere inconsistency between, say, the Scotland Act and a later statute would not compel the courts to conclude that the latter was intended impliedly to repeal the former.

A full answer to this question would also require discussion of the Court of Appeal decision in *R (Jackson) v H.M. Attorney General* (2005), where supporters of hunting challenged the validity of the Hunting Act 2004. The 2004 Act was enacted under the Parliament Acts 1911 and 1949. The 1949 Act amended the 1911 Act, reducing the delaying power of the House of Lords from two years to one. It was itself enacted under the 1911 Act. The applicants argued that the 1949 Act was *ultra vires*, on the grounds that the 1911 Act, as enacted by the Commons, Lords and Sovereign, did not authorise the Commons and Sovereign acting alone to relax the conditions on which their power to act alone had been granted. Accordingly, any statute enacted pursuant to the 1949 Act was itself invalid. The Court of Appeal held that the 1911 Act did permit of its own amendment to the extent contained in the 1949 Act. Four statutes had been enacted under the amended Parliament Act procedure since 1949, and this gave the provisions of the 1949 Act the status of "political fact". Yet the Court of Appeal was not prepared to go any further than this. It observed that the 1911 Act had effected a radical constitutional resettlement in removing the power of the House of Lords, in given circumstances, to block legislation approved by the Commons. Quoting Lord Pearce in *Bribery Commissioner v Ranasinghe* (1965), the Court of Appeal held that such a constitutional settlement might be altered or amended if the regulating instrument (*i.e.* the 1911 Act) so provides and if the terms of its provisions are complied with. Whether or not this is so depends on the proper construction of the regulating instrument. While the Court of Appeal were able to find that the limited alteration to the time-limits effected under the 1911 Act in 1949 was within the scope of the 1911 Act properly construed, there are limitations on the competence of Parliament as redefined for the purposes of the 1911 Act which the courts have jurisdiction to enforce (even, implicitly, to the extent of striking down legislation enacted outwith that sphere of competence). The Diceyan answer to this is that "Parliament" as redefined in the 1911 and 1949 Acts is not, in fact, "Parliament" at all but a delegate thereof (and the Court of Appeal appeared to accept the applicants' submission that legislation passed under the Parliament Acts had the character of delegated legislation). We are not therefore driven to conclude that the courts might now "question or set aside" legislation enacted by Parliament properly so-called, namely the Commons, the Lords and the Sovereign.

The view taken in this book, and suggested here, then, is that provided Parliament speaks clearly, it remains free to make or unmake any law whatever, and although the courts may pronounce on the compatibility of its enactments with Community law or the Convention rights (at Parliament's own behest), they cannot set those enactments aside. There have been adjustments in our understanding of the Diceyan doctrine of parliamentary supremacy, but not such as to deprive that doctrine of its status as the "top rule" of the constitution.

"I think that the day will come when it will be more widely recognised that *Wednesbury* was an unfortunately retrogressive decision in English administrative law, insofar as it suggested that there are degrees of unreasonableness and that only a very extreme degree can bring an administrative decision within the legitimate scope of judicial invalidation" (*R v Secretary of State for the Home Department, ex parte Daly* (2001), *per* Lord Cooke). *Discuss*.

This question invites you to consider the principle of *Wednesbury* unreasonableness (which, despite Lord Cooke's reference to English administrative law, is equally a part of the administrative law of Scotland). Plainly his Lordship is no admirer of the doctrine. You would need to address the weaknesses of the doctrine (and its strengths, if any), and you would also need to ask whether the deficiencies perceived by Lord Cooke have been addressed, adequately or at all, by modifications made to the *Wednesbury* principle in recent cases and, in particular, by the reception of the principle of proportionality. As a general point, note that exam questions on judicial review, whether in "problem" form or discussion questions such as this, give you an opportunity to show off a knowledge and understanding (if you have them) of the extensive case law.

Begin with the *Wednesbury* principle itself. It holds that a court on review should not interfere with an administrative decision on substantive grounds (as distinct from procedural grounds or those grounds of review bound up in the concept of illegality) unless the decision is so unreasonable that no reasonable decision maker in the same circumstances could possibly have come to it. The threshold for intervention is pitched at this level because, provided a decision maker has acted within the four corners of the jurisdiction conferred on him (whether by Parliament or otherwise) and has arrived at the decision in a fair manner, it is not for the courts to question the merits of the outcome other than in an extreme case.

In many circumstances, this hands-off approach was (and remains) appropriate. For example, high-level decisions on social and economic policy are not strictly scrutinised, partly because as a matter of relative expertise the courts should defer to the judgment of the primary decision-maker and partly because democratic processes provide a better channel of accountability for such decisions: see, e.g. *Nottinghamshire County Council v Secretary of State for the Environment* (1986), *East Kilbride District Council v Secretary of State for Scotland* (1995). In other areas, however, the degree of deference apparently required by the *Wednesbury* principle may not be appropriate. Where fundamental human rights are affected by a decision, for example, there are strong arguments for more rigorous scrutiny by the courts.

In *R v Secretary of State for the Home Department, ex parte Brind* (1991), the applicants sought to persuade the House of Lords that in such cases the proper standard of substantive review was not the *Wednesbury* standard, but the principle of proportionality. This doctrine requires a decision maker to show a reasonable relationship between means and ends; or, to put the matter another way, to show that the decision was taken in furtherance of a legitimate aim and that any adverse impact on individuals was no greater than necessary to achieve that aim. The House of Lords declined to adopt a principle of proportionality in that case, but the majority at least did not rule out its future reception. In any event, even prior to *Brind*, the House of Lords had recognised that, in appropriate cases, the *Wednesbury* principle would need to be applied in a stricter way: see *Bugdaycay v Secretary of State for the Home Department* (1987). There, an asylum seeker challenged the decision to return him to his country of origin on the grounds, *inter alia*, that to do so would expose him to a serious risk of being killed. Lord Bridge observed that the right to life is the most fundamental of all human rights and that a decision impacting on that right should attract the most "anxious scrutiny". He continued: "the court must be entitled to subject an administrative decision to the most rigorous examination, to ensure that it is in no way flawed, according to the gravity of the issue which the decision determines." This approach was developed further by the Court of Appeal in *R v Ministry of Defence, ex parte Smith* (1996) ("the more substantial the interference with human rights, the more the court will require by way of justification before it is satisfied that the decision is reasonable") and followed in Scotland in a number of cases, notably *Abdadou v Secretary of State for the Home Department* (1998).

Accordingly, even prior to the entry into force of the Human Rights Act 1998, the courts had developed the *Wednesbury* principle so that it applied variably depending on context and, where human rights were in issue, amounted in many respects to a proportionality test in all but name. Now that the Human Rights Act is in force, the courts are free to apply a proportionality standard in such cases. A number of points may be noted, however. First, even though there may be analytical differences between proportionality and *Wednesbury* (even as developed in *Bugdaycay* and *Smith*), in the majority of cases the outcome will be the same whichever test is applied (see, *e.g.* Lord Slynn in *R v Chief Constable of Sussex, ex parte International Traders' Ferry Limited* (1999), Lord Steyn in *R (Daly) v Secretary of State for the Home Department* (2001)). Secondly, and relatedly, even when applying a test of proportionality in human rights cases, there remain circumstances in which the courts should defer to the judgment of the primary decision maker: see, Lord Hope's discussion of this issue in *R v Director of Public Prosecutions, ex parte Kebilene* (1999) and the comments of Lord Hoffmann in *R (ProLife Alliance) v BBC* (2003). The reception of a proportionality test, in other words, does not do away with the need, implicit in the *Wednesbury* doctrine, for an appropriate division of labour between legislature, executive and the courts. Thirdly, outwith the field of fundamental rights, the ordinary *Wednesbury* standard remains the proper standard of review (see e.g. *R (Medway Council) v Secretary of State for Transport* (2002) and *R (Association of British Civilian Internees—Far Eastern Region) v Secretary of State for Defence* (2003)).

A suggested conclusion is as follows. If the *Wednesbury* test is taken literally, it will not always permit of judicial review of a sufficient intensity to provide proper protection for particular rights and interests we regard as especially deserving of protection. The tendency, in the past, to apply the test in this way may lie at the root of Lord Cooke's disquiet. It is not obvious, however, that the decision in *Wednesbury* was "unfortunately retrograde". The test captures the need for judicial deference to administrative decision making, if it fails to define the circumstances in and extent to which such deference is desirable. Prior to the entry into force of the Human Rights Act, the courts showed themselves able to apply the *Wednesbury* test more flexibly, so that deference was accorded where appropriate and more searching scrutiny applied elsewhere. The express reception of a proportionality doctrine pursuant to the Human Rights Act, alongside the *Wednesbury* test, does not draw a line under the continuing process of calibrating and re-calibrating the intensity of judicial review.

INDEX